Built on a biblical foundation and supplying numerous practical applications, *Faith Legacy for Couples* will help you and your marriage become everything God intended it to be.

—**Drs. Les and Leslie Parrott**, authors of *Love Talk*

In *Faith Legacy for Couples*, Jim and Jerolyn Bogear have provided an inspirational guide and reliable map for your marriage journey. Following the principles they teach in this book will help you leave a legacy of God-honoring, covenant marriage built on biblical values after which your children can pattern their own marriages. In a day when so many marriages are disintegrating, this book is a valuable gift for any couple wanting to build a lasting marriage.

—**Jim Garlow**, senior pastor, Skyline Wesleyan Church

Jim and Jerolyn have written a great book on marriage with fresh thinking that gets to the heart of the matter. They address the practical values that not only make a marriage last, but bring great happiness and meaning to the relationship. With humor, biblical insight, and wise experience, they deliver timeless truth for a couple of any age. I highly recommend it!

—**Dan Reiland**, executive pastor, 12Stone Church;
author of *Amplified Leadership*

People are committed to plenty. Perhaps too much. Yet, Jim and Jerolyn Bogear get the value of the commitment of one man to one woman in the marriage covenant. That is, the personal commitment to Christ and his Word are the key to couples living a lifetime of true faith legacy. *Faith Legacy for Couples* will inspire your relationship with Jesus Christ as well as your commitment to marriage and family.

—**Jim Dunn**, executive director, Church Multiplication
and Discipleship, The Wesleyan Church

Spoiler alert: this book is not for the short-term, faint of heart, fluttery of only emotion seeking romantic. This is a book for the man and woman who want to live life and love fully in the pursuit of a God-honoring, Jesus-loving, children-providing, and generation-impacting marriage. If you want your marriage to be built on time-tested principles and have something worth passing on to your kids' marriages, then *Faith Legacy for Couples* is a great resource for you. Read this book; live it out; and know that you will be helping the marriage of the people who will be raising your grandchildren!

—**John Jackson**, president, William Jessup University
and Leadership; author; speaker

With the same keen insight and honest revelation readers enjoyed in *Faith Legacy: Six Values to Shape Your Child's Journey*, Jim and Jerolyn Bogear offer couples warm light on the path to leaving a legacy. *Faith Legacy for Couples* is clear, practical, and easy to put into practice. Without being formulaic, these authors both challenge and cheer for couples to connect, dream, and build a marriage that influences generations far beyond this one.

—**Michele Cushatt**, author, speaker, coach with
Ken Davis Communications organization

Jim and Jerolyn draw from a deep well of God-inspired experience shaped by their walk of faith. You will be enriched by the nuggets of wisdom they share from their journey. They are modeling the way for couples seeking to follow Christ in their relationships.

—**Henry Smith**, president, Indiana Wesleyan University

FAITH LEGACY
for
COUPLES

Seven Values to Shape Your Marriage

Jim and Jerolyn Bogear

wesleyan
publishing
house

Indianapolis, Indiana

Copyright © 2012 by Jim and Jerolyn Bogear
Published by Wesleyan Publishing House
Indianapolis, Indiana 46250
Printed in the United States of America
ISBN: 978-0-89827-526-1

Library of Congress Cataloging-in-Publication Data

Bogear, Jim.
  Faith legacy for couples : seven values to shape your marriage / Jim and
Jerolyn Bogear.
      p. cm.
  Includes bibliographical references (p.).
  ISBN 978-0-89827-526-1
  1. Marriage--Religious aspects--Christianity. I. Bogear, Jerolyn. II. Title.
  BV835.B63 2012
  248.8'44--dc23
                          2012008292

This book is dedicated first to each other. If we didn't live this out in real life, the vision and values of this book would only be theoretical. To Jerolyn, I (Jim) again renew my vows of covenant marriage and commit to living this book out with you for many more years to come. To Jim, I (Jerolyn) also renew my commitment to our covenant for the rest of our days. I am so proud to be living life with you.

Next we dedicate this book to our wonderful kids, whom we love so dearly, and to their marriages. We trust that our marriage has been a positive model for them to desire to emulate. Our oldest two, Lauren (married to Chris Snider) and Shay (married to Haley Pearson Bogear), have both already made these vows, and we trust they will continue to live out a covenantal marriage. We love our son- and daughter-in-law, Chris and Haley, and are so thankful for both couples' commitment to Christ and one another. As we have attempted to live and model, we pray that you go and live a legacy of a godly, biblical marriage. To Gabby, we continue to desire that you see our marriage as that model to follow so that when you choose your marriage mate, you will live your own legacy of a lifelong marriage covenant.

We also dedicate this book to the memory of Jim's mom and the godly example of his parents' (Ron and Lois) more than fifty-eight years of marriage. Thanks, Dad and Mom Bogear.

Contents

Acknowledgements   9

Introduction   11

Part One: Defining a Marriage

    One: What Is Marriage?   15

    Two: Roles in Marriage   27

    Three: Gender Differences   55

Part Two: The Values of a Covenant Marriage

    Four: Define the Seven Values for Your Marriage   73

    Five: The Marriage Trip   91

Part Three: Strategies for Building Your Marriage

    Six: Strategy 1: Devotion to God   107

    Seven: Strategy 2: Dialogue   120

    Eight: Strategy 3: Demonstrate   137

    Nine: Strategy 4: Delight   158

    Ten: Some Final Thoughts   176

Appendix: Devotions   178

Quarterly Checkup   199

Resources   202

Notes   203

Acknowledgements

We would like to thank all the couples that we have already had the privilege of investing in. We encourage you to build the godly, biblical marriages God desires and designed.

We would also like to thank our publisher, Don Cady. Once the first book was published, Don graciously asked, "Do you have any more books in you?" Thanks, Don, for believing in us. Thanks also to Kevin Scott and the team of editors and marketers at Wesleyan Publishing House. We appreciate your efforts to make this book the best it can become.

We want to thank those who have influenced us by living out what it means to be united as one—taking the marriage covenant seriously enough to model it for us. For many who may never know your impact in shaping our marriage, we thank you.

Introduction

In 2009 our first book, *Faith Legacy: Six Values to Shape Your Child's Journey*, was published. The book idea came out of a rite of passage legacy trip we take with our children when they turn fourteen. On the trip, we review the six values we have tried to instill in them, and then we hand off the baton, so to speak. They must take personal ownership of those values.

Since we've received such a great response, we decided to write *Faith Legacy for Couples* following the same concept. Every healthy marriage begins with two healthy people, rich in value-based living, ready to give themselves to the other for the rest of their lives. They know who they are as individuals in every aspect of life. Together, the man and woman can formulate a life that will be fulfilling and have a positive impact on their world.

It is our prayer that through *Faith Legacy for Couples* you will purposefully establish a plan for growing a strong, healthy marriage that will leave a faith legacy to those who live alongside you and for those still to come. May this be only the beginning.

—Jim and Jerolyn Bogear

part one

DEFINING A MARRIAGE

one

What Is Marriage?

Think back to your wedding day. If you're not married yet, imagine what it will be like. Picture the flowers; the rows of chairs; the people dressed up, eagerly waiting; the presents stacked on a table; the cake waiting to be cut; a bride in white; and a groom in tails. The picture is perfect, and the day is promising and hopeful.

The average American wedding costs around 25,000 dollars. Most often, more time is spent on picking the right dress, choosing bridesmaids' dresses, and arranging flowers than on premarital counseling. I (Jim) had a teacher who said, "Some of you will spend more time shopping for a pair of shoes than you will the person you are planning to spend the rest of your life with." The wedding is a sacred ceremony with a wonderful party to follow, but the marriage is to be for a lifetime. How much more time and energy should we commit to the health of our marriage?

A Sacred Covenant

According to Merriam-Webster, marriage is "the state of being united to a person of the opposite sex as husband or wife in a consensual and contractual relationship recognized by law."[1] While marriage is all these things, it must be more. A "consensual and contractual relationship" does not attend to a spouse lying in a hospital bed dying of cancer. It doesn't hold two people together when they've lost their house or, worse yet, experienced the death of a child. A legal contract provides little comfort or support when the crisis of unemployment and debt hits. If we look at marriage merely as a contract, when times get tough, it is no more sturdy or binding than two pieces of paper held together by a Band-Aid. Fortunately, the Bible offers an alternative perspective on marriage.

Success in marriage happens when there is surrender to Scripture. Read what Jesus had to say about the permanent bond of marriage in Matthew 19:3–6: "Some Pharisees came to [Jesus] to test him. They asked, 'Is it lawful for a man to divorce his wife for any and every reason?' 'Haven't you read,' he replied, 'that at the beginning the Creator "made them male and female,"' and said, "For this reason a man will leave his father and mother and be united to his wife, and the two will become one flesh"?

So they are no longer two, but one. Therefore, what God has joined together, let man not separate.'"

Marriage is more than a contract; it is a covenant between a man and a woman. The Old Testament marriage agreement was a covenant that bound together two people, making them forever associated with the other. It was not entered into flippantly, but with forethought, reverence, and ceremony. Marriage was only one of the kinds of covenants that could be made between two people. Whatever kind of covenant was made, those involved knew it was an unbreakable promise.

In an Old Testament covenant, several rituals were observed to connect the two parties together. They exchanged cloaks (outer garments), so they would look like the other person. They took the other person's name as part of their own name, binding their identities together. In other words, we would have taken the names Jim Jerolyn Bogear and Jerolyn Jim Bogear. These acts and others served to bind their lives together in a covenant that could not be broken and that would last as long as they both lived.[2]

Modern marriages contain similar rituals. We exchange rings symbolizing our commitment to one another. Many women take the man's last name as their own. We live in the same house together. We have children together. Our lives are bound together socially and financially.

What many don't realize is that this marriage covenant between humans is the only one instituted by God. All other family relationships originate from this covenantal relationship of a man and woman in marriage. God created both the man and woman and put them together in this relationship. Every other family relationship—children, parents, aunts, uncles, grandparents, siblings, you name it—all started with this one bond that God put together. God allowed us to procreate and to have a part in "creating" all the other family relationships. But it started with God hand-crafting this covenant of marriage between a man and a woman.

An Unbreakable Trust

The difference between many modern marriages and the sacred covenant of the Bible is that many today have surrendered their unbreakable trust in their marriage partner, while also giving up being the trustworthy partner they promised to be. Marriage hangs on the commitment to trust one another, and trust takes time and intention to build. Entering a marriage without trust is like jumping out of an airplane without a parachute; it lacks common sense. Trust is the foundation of a healthy relationship.

We must first trust ourselves to be the person we promise to be. Entering into a marriage covenant is not like taking a car out for a test drive; if you don't like how it handles, the interior upholstery is uncomfortable, or you want a different color, you choose a different car. You must decide ahead of time to be a person who can be trusted with a commitment to love one other person for the rest of your life. Or if you are married, then you have already entered a covenant; it's time to work on becoming the kind of person you've promised your spouse you would be. When we do premarital counseling, and even during the wedding ceremony, I (Jim) will make the comment to the couple, "For so long you have looked for Mr. or Mrs. Right, but today you are pledging that the looking is over. Today's commitment is to start *being* Mr. or Mrs. Right for your spouse." It is possible to grow in your trustworthiness. But you must choose to do so and put in the time and hard work a singular commitment like marriage requires.

Will you be the kind of person your spouse can trust to be faithful and available no matter what happens? Life throws many curveballs. One of you may become incapacitated or lose your job; you may one day find that there is not enough money in the bank account for the next mortgage payment; or one of your children might become gravely ill. Everyone faces large and small obstacles every day. The question is whether you are going to face them united as a couple or separated by the trials. It's easy to stick with a relationship in the walking on the beach hand-in-hand into the sunset kind of times. But when the road becomes rocky and painful, will you stick it out at your spouse's side with integrity and love? That is what it means to be trustworthy.

Your spouse also needs to be able to trust that you are going to continue growing as a person and to allow him or her to grow as well. Growth is a funny thing. It certainly involves making improvements to your life and character, but it also means repeatedly trying and sometimes failing along the way. A spouse must be able to trust you to not give up, to continue to improve yourself, to let him or her have the freedom to grow as well, and to be patient with each other's failures while you're doing it. When we get married, many of us have an image in mind of what a perfect spouse would be like. In the beginning stages of love, we may even see our spouse as exemplifying that perfection. But with time and experience, reality sets in, and we begin to see the flaws and humanity of our spouse. This presents a challenge. As Bill Cosby said, "That married couples can live together day after day is a miracle that the Vatican has overlooked."[3]

Many people react to their spouse's flaws in one of two ways: (1) They become disillusioned with the marriage and walk away completely, saying that it was a complete mistake in the first place; or (2) they nag and complain about their spouse's shortcomings until the spouse either begins to conform to the ideal image in their mind (unlikely) or begins to shut down and eventually walk away (more likely). Fortunately, there is a third and superior way for dealing with the flaws you find in your spouse: You can love and accept your spouse with all the flaws and imperfections, patiently loving as he or she grows into the person God created him or her to be. It sometimes makes it easier if you remember that your spouse is living with an imperfect person as well; be thankful that he or she chose to love you in spite of your short-comings.

A trustworthy spouse offers unconditional love and a safe place where an imperfect human being can exist without the constant pressure of conforming to an unrealistic image. I (Jerolyn) struggled with having unrealistic expectations for many years. I would expect my husband to be practically perfect as a human being and flawless in everything he did. What a horribly high bar to set for any human being—a standard that is virtually unreachable. There is certainly a time to offer your spouse constructive feedback and to challenge one another to grow, but it must always be done as a team working toward the same goal, in a loving manner and filled with grace.

In a healthy relationship, trust goes beyond you being trustworthy. Have you chosen to trust your spouse? If not, why? Notice that we deliberately chose the word *chosen*. Trust does not just happen. It is not the product of Hollywood-style romance and it does not arise from a fleeting feeling or notion. In addition to being a trustworthy person, you must make a conscious decision to trust the person you have chosen to be bound to in a marriage covenant.

Placing trust in another person is a huge step of faith. Perhaps you remember the movie *Indiana Jones and the Last Crusade*, where Harrison Ford's character was following the directions of an ancient legend to find the Holy Grail. At one point, he had to step off a ledge into what looked like a bottomless chasm. He had to literally take a leap of faith. And when he did, he stepped onto a camouflaged bridge.[4] You are seeking the Holy Grail of a healthy, thriving, vibrant, loving marriage. But to find it, you have to trust in the person to whom you are making this lifelong commitment. It is a huge step of faith. However, it doesn't have to be completely blind.

Hopefully, when you chose your mate, you looked for qualities that were virtuous and would complement your personality and character—to help make you a better person. Hopefully you found someone whose life and character you could enhance as well. I (Jerolyn) remember asking my mom when I was thirteen how I could know if I had found the right man to marry. She said, "You should have approval from family and friends who are close to you and who know you best and feel a peace from God that he is the right one." I think she gave good advice. Sometimes in the throes of deep affection, your discernment meter can go on the fritz. That is when you need the people closest to you, who know you the best, to offer wisdom and guidance. You might say you believe you can trust this person for the rest of your life, but that may only be desire talking. An objective viewpoint will help you to see your future spouse through clear lenses.

But you must also seek peace from the Father. Only he knows the truth about a person's heart and the future that you as a couple might have together. If you are truly diligent in seeking the will of the Father, you will seek his guidance in choosing the one with whom you will spend the rest of your life.

Once the choice is made, there can be no going back. You must learn to place your trust in the person you married. In the Bible, Ruth made a remarkable commitment to her mother-in-law: "Where you go I will go, and where you stay I will stay. Your people will be my people and your God my God. Where you die I will die, and there I will be buried. May the LORD deal with me, be it ever so severely, if anything but death separates you and me" (Ruth 1:16–17). While this is obviously not a marriage commitment, it is still a tremendous example of trust between two people.

In a healthy marriage, the paths of two people travel side by side for as long as they live; nothing and no one will ever come between them. A biblical, covenant marriage is one man and one woman agreeing to a nonnegotiable, bomb-proof, never-ending, no one, no-how coming between us, I will grow old with you in the nursing home, I will stand by you in a wealthy country club or in the soup line, stuck to you, laughing and crying with you forever kind of covenantal marriage. That is a marriage that is surrendered to Scripture. One spouse trusts the other who handles the family finances. One spouse trusts the other who makes the decisions regarding the direction the family will take. Each spouse trusts the other to live by the values they have agreed to embrace. They trust one another to raise their children as they have agreed to raise them. They trust that, even though temptations may abound in the workplace or elsewhere, both will remain faithful to one another. They trust that someday they will be sitting next to each other in matching rockers, growing old together.

That kind of trust is not earned in a moment, but every day, through seemingly small, insignificant actions that build a foundation of trust on which the marriage can stand. In the chapters ahead, we will discuss ways to build trust in one another and create an impenetrable, covenant marriage. Your marriage will not always be easy and smooth sailing. Claire Cloninger described marriage in this way: "I figure that the degree of difficulty in combining two lives ranks somewhere between rerouting a hurricane and finding a parking place in downtown Manhattan."[5] But there are many ways you can protect your covenant marriage from harm. So, do the work, walk in trust, and live the commitment of your covenant marriage.

As I (Jim) type this, I am watching a man gently caress his wife and dote over her to make sure she is well cared for and loved. It is his wife of fifty-eight years. She is in her last days, and he is, as he always has been, by her side as she has his. She is tired. He is tired. But they are full of love for one another. Together they have walked through life. Perfectly? No. As with all marriages, there have been many flaws and faults. But has it been a biblical marriage? Absolutely. They have been a model of what a covenant marriage looks like. Would I want my marriage to look exactly like theirs? Maybe not exactly, but so much of what I desire for my marriage, they do have. I pray that Jerolyn and I will be able to grow old together, and while we sit across from one another in wheelchairs, I will still know she is everything I could desire in a wife, and that she is mine. My eyes tear up as I type, because the couple I am watching is my mom and dad, loving each other without a word being spoken, but simply with a touch. They have left a legacy of a covenant marriage lived out to its completion.

Next Steps

Questions to Discuss with Your Spouse

1. What does the word *marriage* mean to you?

2. Why did you choose to marry me?

Activities

1. Read together Scripture you can find on marriage. Start with Ephesians 5:21–31; 1 Corinthians 7:1–8; Genesis 2; Matthew 6:19–21; 19:1–4; and Colossians 3:1–17.

2. Find couples who have been married longer than you and ask what marriage means to them.

Roles in Marriage

There was a perfect man who met a perfect woman. After a perfect courtship, they had a perfect wedding. Their life together was, as you might guess, perfect.

One snowy, stormy Christmas Eve, this perfect couple was driving along a winding road when they noticed someone at the roadside in distress. Being the perfect couple, they stopped to help. There stood Santa Claus with a huge bundle of toys. Not wanting to disappoint any children on the eve of Christmas, they loaded Santa and his toys into their vehicle. Soon they were driving along delivering the toys. Unfortunately, the driving conditions deteriorated and the perfect couple and Santa Claus had an accident. Only one of them survived the accident. Who was the survivor?

Answer: The perfect woman. She's the only one that really existed in the first place. Everyone knows there is no Santa Claus or perfect man.

A Man's Response: So, if there is no perfect man or Santa Claus, the perfect woman must have been driving. This explains why there was a car accident.

OK, all kidding aside, there are no perfect women or men. But everyone and everything in life has a role to play. Our doctors watch over our health; our dishwashers clean our dishes; our dogs give us love and companionship; our cars take us where we want to go; our children worship the ground we walk on. OK, maybe not the last one. Still, everyone and everything in life has a purpose and job to do. The same is true within a marriage. We each have roles we must play and others we choose.

In the course of our marriage, we've learned to work together in the roles we have based on our personalities. One thing I (Jim) have learned is that when Jerolyn says, "I have been thinking," it means, "I am expecting us to go get what we need and make it happen today." When we were first married, I didn't get this. We were only planning to live in our first apartment for a few more months as I was finishing graduate school before we accepted our first ministry position. It didn't matter. She wanted to paint the apartment, and I agreed. We dove into this task together, and although we never, ever talk divorce, I wasn't convinced that both of us would come out alive from this one. What was the problem—besides the fact that I hate to paint and probably had a bad attitude? We hadn't learned to work together, didn't know what we were doing, and were both so stubborn that we each were convinced our way was best.

We learned a lot that day. In over twenty-six years of marriage, we've figured out how we work best together. Jerolyn created an excellent word picture of how our marriage works, and how we work together. It's like a child's coloring picture. I throw out an idea of what the picture should look like—a vision, loud and big all over the place. Jerolyn comes in and draws the lines and begins to bring clarity to the picture. I then come back splashing in lots of color, and she finishes by cleaning up where I colored outside the lines of the picture for a completed image of what we desired. Not every marriage works this way, but it's what works for us. Part of growing in your marriage relationship is discovering how you best work together and celebrating that unique design in your marriage. Author Dave Meurer said, "A great marriage is not when the 'perfect couple' comes together. It is when an imperfect couple learns to enjoy their differences."[1] You were each designed to be special, unique individuals. Now you just need to figure out how two unique people are going to live and work together through the rest of your lives. What a great adventure!

Since people are so complex, we can't cover all the ins and outs of the roles a husband and wife will play in a marriage. Diverse personalities and gifts only serve to increase the complexity. But before we tackle the seven values of a biblical marriage, it's important to say a few words about the roles God gives the man and woman in a marriage, as well as some of the differences between sexes (in the next chapter). We'll let Jim speak to the men first, and then Jerolyn to the women.

A Word from Jim to the Men

Men, we need and are called to take the lead in our marriage relationships. Most wives actually want their husbands to take leadership in the home. And I believe the Bible teaches that God has designed men to be the spiritual leaders and providers for the family. It does not mean we must be the only financial provider or even the one making the most money. It does mean that we are the protectors of our homes and defenders of our families.

To "man up" means we take our responsibility seriously and give leadership to our homes. Too often we have abdicated this responsibility. Even though we may be there physically, it is easy to detach emotionally and find other ways to fill our days, hoping that our wives will carry the marriage and provide a foundation for our families. That's not the way God intended it to be.

Let's look at some ways we should man up and take responsibility and leadership in our marriages and homes.

Spiritual Leader

As the spiritual leader, you set the culture of your home. If you and your wife are going to follow Judeo-Christian values, you, the husband, are the one to establish those values for your family. Ephesians 5 describes the basics of what such a home looks like. Love is the central theme in such a home, and sin or anything of darkness is forbidden to reside there. We are children of the light, and the man is responsible to take the leadership in maintaining that light in his home. He is to be guided by wisdom and soberness, following God's example. It is the man's role as the spiritual leader to provide the security and protection of his wife and family with the Word of God.

The Bible compares the marriage relationship to the relationship between Christ and the church, with Christ as the husband and the church as the bride. To understand the analogy, we must understand the role of the priest. Jesus is our high priest, and we cannot replace him, but we can follow his example as the spiritual leader or "priest" of our homes. The book of Hebrews says that "we do not have a high priest who is unable to sympathize with our weaknesses, but we have one who has been tempted in every way" (4:15). Jesus is without sin, and even though we certainly are not without sin, we are still to give priestly leadership to our wives as Christ does for the church.

As the husband, you must lead, setting the example and creating the spiritual environment of your home. For example, my wife and children need to see me reading Scripture and praying. I can talk about God all I want, but if they are not able to observe an active relationship between God and me, my words are empty.

I'm the first to admit that I do not do a good job of this all the time, but praying with your spouse is a great way to lead. Jerolyn and I continue to work at it. I pray *for* her regularly; I need to pray *with* her more. Something we do well is having spiritual discussions. These happen on a regular basis. We talk about what God is doing in and around us; what he is teaching us and how we can grow spiritually. I also need to be my wife's most devoted accountability partner and she mine.

Being the spiritual leader means getting the family involved in a local body of believers. Corporate worship and community service are a vital part of spiritual growth and living a life of significance. "Let us hold unswervingly to the hope we profess, for he who promised is faithful. And let us consider how we may spur one another on toward love and good deeds. Let us not give up meeting together, as some are in the habit of doing, but let us encourage one another—and all the more as you see the Day approaching" (Heb. 10:23–25). The man's role is to take the first step in directing his family through the church doors—not just to sit, but to get involved. Working together in a church is a great way for a couple to grow together.

When the Israelites built the temple, the high priest went annually into the Holy of Holies (where the presence of God lived) to make atonement for the sins of the people. The high priest had to prepare himself physically and spiritually before he was clean enough to enter to meet with the Almighty. This included bathing just before entering and putting on linen undergarments, a linen tunic, a linen sash, and a turban — sacred garments (Lev. 16:3–4).

As the spiritual leader of your home, your wife needs to know you are trustworthy in leading her to the throne of God. She needs the assurance that her spiritual well-being is of such great importance that you are ready to defend the gospel and her right to worship. Risks may have to be taken and stands be made. The husband must stand ready to do just that. Following Christ is not always the popular or easy route to take. But it's time to man up and lead the way on the right path. Your wife's spiritual well-being is counting on you.

First Timothy 3:4–5 states that an overseer must "manage his own family well and see that his children obey him with proper respect. (If anyone does not know how to manage his own family, how can he take care of God's church?)." An elder's home life is an essential consideration. Before he can lead in the church he must demonstrate his spiritual leadership within the context of his family.

"The Greek word translated 'manages' means 'to preside' or 'to have authority over.' The same Greek word is translated 'rule' in [1 Timothy] 5:17 in reference to elders leading in the church. An elder's ability to rule the church is affirmed in his home. Therefore he must be a strong spiritual leader there before he is qualified to lead in the church."[2]

These principles go beyond men who want to be leaders in the church. A clear message for men is that if we are not leading well in our marriages and homes, we are not leading well anyplace.

If we cannot give spiritual leadership in our homes, we cannot expect to help lead others well. What are you doing to help your wife mature in her faith? What kind of environment are you creating of spiritual hunger and vitality in your home? Ephesians 5 says, "Husbands, love your wives, just as Christ loved the church and gave himself up for her to make her holy, cleansing her by the washing with water through the word, and to present her to himself as a radiant church, without stain or wrinkle or any other blemish, but holy and blameless" (vv. 25–27).

Are we husbands loving and leading our wives by creating a culture of spiritual health and vitality in our homes? How are we sharing spiritual matters and giving leadership?

Both the 1 Timothy and Ephesians passages are clear: Before we can be spiritual leaders *anywhere*, we must be spiritual leaders in our marriages! This is the indicator, the starting point, the place where we, as husbands, must win first in the area of leading well. Spiritual leadership begins and ends with doing so in our marriages and homes.

Protector

No matter how weak or strong your wife is, she is looking for you to be her protector. As men, we are generally the physically stronger sex. We are built to protect our wives and families. But protecting our wives goes far beyond brute and bronze. There are three basic ways in which a husband needs to protect his wife—financially, physically, and emotionally.

Financially. For those who think I am heading in the direction of the "me, Tarzan; you, Jane," grab her by the hair, and "me hunt for food" stereotype, let me clarify: Wrong! My mom worked long before I was around, long after I left home, and all the years in between. She also handled the checkbook and managed the money; but Dad was clearly the protector. Dad didn't sit at home or spend the dollars Mom earned. And if money was tight, it was Dad who worked the second job for years or picked up odd jobs to protect and provide for his family. There was no question about where the burden of responsibility fell. Dad has often said that because Mom worked, we were able to afford the simple things we had. We did not have a lot, but we never felt like we were without. We never knew we were poor because Dad made sure to provide.

You see, it isn't how much either of you makes, but rather who takes the responsibility of protecting you financially as you walk through various decisions in providing for your family's needs. Maybe as the husband, you fix things. You save dollars and protect your family financially by doing it yourself. You make sure the car is fixed or the house is repaired. I do not fix things. Jerolyn actually does more of that than I do. But if something is broken, I try to make sure that someone takes care of, fixes, or replaces it. I don't have to do it myself; I just have to make sure, as protector, it is being handled.

If Jerolyn chose to return to work outside the home, she could probably earn more than me. I would laugh every payday. But it is my responsibility as a husband to protect our family by taking care of the financial needs. Again, the amount of money isn't the issue.

> Many men rule their home but don't rule it very well—
> they don't get the desired results. By implication, a man's
> home includes his resources. A man may be spiritually and
> morally qualified to be an elder, be skilled in teaching, and
> have a believing wife and children who follow his leader-
> ship in the home, but if he doesn't rule his household well
> in the financial realm, he is disqualified from spiritual
> leadership. Stewardship of possessions is a critical test of
> a man's leadership. His home is the proving ground where
> his leadership capabilities can be clearly demonstrated.[3]

This passage is speaking to those who may desire to be a leader in the church. But again, allow me to reiterate that if we are not being the spiritual leader in all aspects, including providing finan-cially for our wives, then we will not lead well anywhere. To finan-cially provide is part of being the spiritual leader and assuming the responsibility God has placed on us. So often we want to have the title of leader but do not want the responsibility of that leader-ship. Here, the title is husband, and as such, we are to lead our wives in the area of financially providing for their needs.

Physically. Too many men are leaving. I am not talking about literally leaving their wives, although there is way too much of that going on. I'm talking about failing to be physically present for their wives. Proverbs 27:8 says, "Like a bird that strays from its nest is a man who strays from his home." Physical presence is vital to the health of a marriage. We men need to stay in the nest.

We have all heard women say, "I don't want you to work more; we have enough of your money. What I want is more of you!" We husbands sometimes think that if we provide more for our wives, they'll love and respect us more. In reality, they just want more of us.

We have talked about being the protector of our marriages in a variety of roles and responsibilities, but being physically present is often the neglected one. Usually it's not that we're against spending time with our wives; many of us just don't realize that our presence is a huge statement of love to them. Of course, there are men who simply do not want to be at home. They work all day and come home to a nagging, caustic environment. (Jerolyn will address that with the wives.) But the environment of the home is a team effort between the husband and wife. You, husband, can't pass off the responsibility; it is still on you to be at home.

Before we can ever be the protector emotionally, we have to be there physically. We cannot phone this one in, guys. Many of us have said, "I'm not out doing things with the guys or hanging in places I should't be. I'm even doing healthy things like activities and hobbies; I am working for you." Really? Are you working for her or avoiding being at home? Are you working harder and longer for her, or are you trying to build up your reputation so you can climb the corporate ladder? Are you working harder for her, or are you fulfilling an insecure need to show others how hard you work?

This is not some kind of revolution to call all men to stop working. We all need to work. But I have battled this drive in myself for a long time. It's easy for me to feel guilty for being at home and not working, but not so much the other way around. I'm wrestling a desire both to provide and to prove. A very strong work ethic is something I wholeheartedly believe in, but it can become a detriment to my marriage. There needs to be a balance. What if I started feeling a little guiltier about being at work more than being at home? What if my work ethic carried into my marriage?

Again, the first issue for many of us is to be at home rather than every other place. The excuse may be work, but many of us also allow our hobbies and time with friends to take away from our time with our wives. I love to play golf. When we were first married, and into our first ministry in Columbus, Ohio, I would think and dream about being out playing golf, even when I wasn't. When I could, I would get away after work to go practice my game even if only for forty-five minutes to an hour. It consumed my brain. Golf, while in no way bad in and of itself, became all-consuming—playing, practicing, thinking about playing, dreaming about playing, or wishing I was playing, rather than doing whatever it was I was doing. Now I could have said that, after all, I was only practicing golf. I may have been gone for a while, but I wasn't at a bar or hanging with the guys and doing things that were wrong or harmful. But the addiction of it caused me to *not* be there physically for my wife. And that was wrong.

Why would I be so selfish as to not want to be with my wife and instead out doing something on my own? Again, a hobby is not bad, but when priorities are misplaced, that action or activity becomes wrong. Playing a round of golf with the boys or my wife having a night out with the girls is not bad; in fact, it's healthy for all. The fact that golf was more important to me than being physically present with my wife was a major issue. I had to repent and reprioritize.

If work or a hobby is distracting you from spending more valuable time with your wife, changes need to happen. You are involved in a two-person marriage, and both people must be present for it to work. Work hard to provide for your family. Take time to relax and enjoy your hobbies. But prioritize your time so that your wife gets the best of you—be physically and fully present.

The church is the bride of Christ, and no matter how much the church has messed up or let Christ down, Christ has never left! We must follow his example. No matter what, our wives must know we are there for them.

Emotionally. While your wife desperately wants you to be physically involved in your marriage, it means nothing if you are not also emotionally engaged in the relationship. Your wife is not looking for a hangout buddy. She wants to connect with you on a much deeper level. Don't just say that you care for her; show her by looking her in the face and allowing her to see who you really are. Don't allow her to simply hope that you will someday invest emotionally in this relationship; take time to be there. Listen and engage your heart and mind.

We have all seen or heard about men being physically present but emotionally absent. How many times did we see our own dads sit in a recliner, never engaging with our moms? Oh, we men will often think how well we are doing, since we're not like our neighbors who are out going to places they don't belong, but we can be just as ineffective in our marital relationships if we are not truly there for our wives. We may be sitting at home, but our minds and hearts are out with the boys, watching TV, on the Internet, or otherwise disengaged. An emotional connection is what our wives need! As in all other areas of our marriages, this isn't about us. Marriage is about completely investing in our wives.

Negative emotions can often be more harmful than withholding positive emotional engagement. Ever tried walking on eggshells? It's not easy, and it's impossible to not break some. That's what was happening at our house for some time. It wasn't constant, but it was often enough that Jerolyn had to tell me that the family didn't know how to act around me: "Whatever happened today has caused you to react negatively to everything we say and do. Your attitude is not right, and we feel like we are walking on eggshells around you." Ouch! I hated that because I often wouldn't know or believe how I was coming across. It took a hard look for me to receive this, seek forgiveness, and ask for help to be better. Too many of us, when we do show up, create a culture of eggshell-walking for our wives. While your wife wants you to be honest about what is happening in your life, she doesn't need you to take your frustrations out on her. Let her support you, but don't make her your emotional punching bag.

Men, let me remind you that your wives *want* the security of your love and relationship. The emotional attachment is huge. How does a woman spell love? S-E-C-U-R-I-T-Y, T-R-U-S-T, and T-E-N-D-E-R-N-E-S-S. I guarantee that if you provide the emotional protection, she will love you and meet your needs. This is so critical. She needs to know you are "all in" with your commitment to building a strong, healthy marriage. She needs to know you are doing your best to meet her needs and to emotionally surrender yourself to her. She needs to know you will celebrate the smallest of things, but even more, that you will determine to simply celebrate your life with her. She needs to know that you will communicate honestly and transparently. Then and only then will your wife trust you and allow for an emotional intimacy like you never dreamed. This is not a theory but a practical, truthful reality!

So first, make it a priority to be there physically. But second, when you are there for your wife, be there completely. Don't spend time at home only to never engage with your wife. Find a balance. Your wife not only needs you to be present physically, but mentally and emotionally, as well. Strive to always be fully present.

A Word from Jerolyn to the Women

God created women in a unique design that helps us fulfill our part of the marriage covenant. Like men, we are made in God's image, but God gave us special gifts that complement and enhance the image of God in men. You are beautifully made to significantly fulfill every task that God calls you to do. I was reading today in Exodus where God gave instructions to build and furnish the tabernacle. In describing one of the workers, it says, "I have filled him with the Spirit of God, with skill, ability and knowledge in all kinds of crafts" (Ex. 31:3). God will also give you every skill you need to fulfill your task as a wife. He values you just as he made you and desires for you to see value in yourself and your marriage.

Respecter

One of the most important roles a woman can play in her marriage is that of respecter. That's because one of man's greatest needs is for respect. We will talk about this more in the next chapter, but if a man does not have the respect of his wife, he feels as if he has no worth in her eyes. A wife can build up her husband and encourage him to reach his greatest potential by giving him the respect he needs and deserves as the heads of the homes.

Respect is a matter of the heart. You determine by your will whether to respect another person or not. If you have trouble respecting your husband, it is a matter of the heart. Either your pride hinders you from granting him the respect he deserves, or he is not living in such a way as to earn your respect. If the latter is the case, seek God's redemption for your husband. Pray for him to seek God's love and healing in his life. But your husband's need for redemption does not get you off the hook in terms of showing respect. You must still continue to show God's love and compassion to your husband. This is not easy and can only be done by the power of the Holy Spirit and with a humble heart. Ultimately, we can't change our husbands or how they behave. But we *can* seek change in our own hearts and behaviors.

Respect for your husband is shown in two primary ways: how you talk *to* your husband, and how you talk *about* your husband. If you are unable to speak to your husband in a loving and respectful tone, you have a heart issue—whether it's your pride or his need for redemption. Both require humility. You can't expect to receive the respect and love you desire if your words to or about your husband are dripping with disdain. This can often come in the form of nagging. Journalist Elizabeth Bernstein recently shared her definition: "Nagging—the interaction in which one person repeatedly makes a request, the other person repeatedly ignores it and both become increasingly annoyed—is an issue every couple will grapple with at some point. While the word itself can provoke chuckles and eye-rolling, the dynamic can potentially be as dangerous to a marriage as adultery or bad finances. Experts say it is exactly the type of toxic communication that can eventually sink a relationship."[4] The old adage that words can never harm us really isn't so true after all. There is incredible power in our words and in the way we use them to build up or tear down. Though women are often associated with nagging, men can slip into nagging as well; or they can ignore their wife's requests, leading to frustration and more nagging. We each deserve to be honored with loving, patient, and gentle words.

I think wives often come into a marriage thinking they will change the parts of their husbands they don't like. Your husband will never be your ideal. He may grow into a better version of himself, but who you married is who you get. Journalist Sydney J. Harris said, "If mates 'change' after marriage, it is only in the direction they were already headed, not in the direction that the other may have hoped for."[5] So in this process of trying to mold your husband into the Prince Charming you think you deserve, you devalue the unique individual God made him to be, and you are falsely elevating yourself to a place of superiority. Remember, for every one of those things you want to change in your husband, there is something that could be changed about yourself too.

As a wife, you must come to a place of complete and unconditional acceptance of your husband. It is only in this attitude of the heart that you can speak to and about your husband in a loving and respectful manner or learn to keep quiet when you need to be quiet. (Remember, you don't have to say *everything* that comes to mind.) Building up your husband with your words builds him up in his mind as well. He feels good about what he is doing, and your words will encourage him to want to do even greater things and be an even better person. Remember Proverbs 31:12: "She brings him good, not harm, all the days of her life."

Submitter

The wife is the submitter. Yes, I used the "S" word. Too often people shy away from discussing submission because many believe it to be demeaning to women. After the women's liberation movement of the 1970s, the subject of submission became taboo. But actually, submission is misunderstood. Since it's a biblical principle, we must address it.

Submission is not a weak position; quite the opposite. It takes a strong person to yield to the leadership of another and carry the burdens of the position. The word *submit* in the Greek is *hupotasso*, meaning "to arrange under, to subordinate, to subject, put in subjection, to subject one's self, obey, to submit to one's control, to yield to one's admonition or advice, to obey, be subject." In the military it meant to be placed under another's command. In the non-military, submit meant "a voluntary attitude of giving in, cooperating, assuming responsibility, and carrying a burden."[6] Notice that submission to your husband is a willing, voluntary action. You choose to yield to your husband as the leader of your home. You are not placed there in bondage, but in freedom. He is put in the position as head of the home, and you are placed under the head; not to be dominated, but protected.

But your submission is not passive. You are given responsibilities. You have burdens to carry. Author and speaker Charles

Swindoll said, "[My wife] was not designed to be my echo, a little vanilla shadow curled up in a corner, awaiting my next order. She was designed by God to be my counterpart, a necessary and needed individual to help me become all God wanted me to be."[7] And frankly, I am so glad that I'm the wife and not the husband. I would never want to carry the burdens Jim carries as the head of our marriage and home. While the wife has responsibilities in her position, the place of leadership carries even greater burdens.

The wonder of submission lies in Ephesians 5:23 and 25, where the husband is admonished to love and care for the wife as Christ loves and cares for the church. Now that is a tremendous responsibility. Christ gave his life for the church, and your husband is to be willing to give his life for you in every decision and on every path where he leads your family. All aspects of his leadership are to be done out of love and respect for you, the bride.

Submission is not a weak position of cowering to another's whims, but one of yielding to the authority God has placed over us for protection and guidance, just as Christ loves and guides his church. Your husband carries a tremendous burden of responsibility, and he needs your support to stand strong. Author Susan T. Foh puts it like this: "Problems with the hierarchical model for marriage arise only when husband and/or wife are disobeying God's Word. The husband is commanded to nourish and cherish his wife, and so his decisions should be qualified by concern for his wife's best interests. When the husband obeys God's commands, the wife suffers no hardship through her submission to him."[9]

Tone Setter

Another role for the wife is the tone setter. She is the one who sets the tone of the home. Her demeanor and how she carries herself will establish the demeanor of the home. Even if the wife is not the dominant personality, how she handles herself around the dominant personalities and her response to them will be the tone of the home. There is no scientific backing to this observation; it is simply that, an observation. But Proverbs 31 will back me up: "She is clothed with strength and dignity; she can laugh at the days to come. She speaks with wisdom, and faithful instruction is on her tongue" (vv. 25–26).

I don't claim to have Proverbs 31 down. In fact, one of my favorite quotes is by mystery writer Catherine Aird: "If you can't be a good example, then you'll just have to be a horrible warning."[10] And I have a lot of data to draw from. On numerous occasions when I have had a bad attitude or spoken unkindly to my family, I have changed the mood of the entire household. It's a strange phenomenon that surprises me every time. It goes back to the common adage, "If the wife ain't happy, ain't nobody happy." Unfortunately, that is only too true, and we women carry a responsibility as wives to maintain a pleasant atmosphere in our homes.

We can all list the characteristics of a healthy, happy home: kindness, laughter, cooperation, positive attitudes, and integrity.

And we all know examples of the attitudes and atmosphere of an unhealthy home. Often we can take personal responsibility for establishing such an atmosphere. For example, how many of us have started nagging our husbands the minute they walk in the door. We've been saving up all day, adding to our list until they get in the door. Then we hit them with a barrage of complaints. King Solomon described us well: "A quarrelsome wife is like a constant dripping on a rainy day; restraining her is like restraining the wind or grasping oil with the hand" (Prov. 27:15–16). That's not how I want my husband to describe me — as an annoying drip. It's not exactly the happily ever after I was looking for. So how do you establish a positive atmosphere in the home? It starts with your identity.

A woman's identity is not defined by her circumstances or the roles she lives. What if we should lose our husband or children? If our identity is completely tied to them, who are we without them? Besides, when we define ourselves by our roles, we place our identity in the hands of others. For example, what if the following statements were true:

- When my children misbehave, it's a reflection on me as a parent.
- When my husband makes a bad decision, it means I did a bad job of choosing a spouse.
- If my husband is unfaithful, I am not worth being loved unconditionally.

When we view our roles as the definition of who we are, we set a trap for ourselves.

But the Bible has a much better way to define us—as children of God. When I identify who I am first and foremost in the light of Jesus Christ, I am not an action or a role. I'm a child who is valued and loved by the Almighty. In this skin, I can view my circumstances as just that—temporary conditions of my surroundings. Who I am does not change because of them. My house may change; my job may change; and what state I live in may change. But the person God has created me to be will always exist and grow into a better version of who I was all along. I will be a created being who lives for the glory of my Lord.

It is in this state of mind that we establish ourselves to be exactly who God designed us to be. There is no pressure to be a positive reflection of another person. We are who we are with all of our failures and successes. And that alone will create an atmosphere of hope and joy that will lead our families to work hard together. We no longer have the fear of failure or rejection because the foundation is established that our family unit is working hard together and accepting each person just as they are in their contribution to the family.

And it is you who holds this key. You have the ability to create a safe haven for your husband and make him feel rested and welcome in his home. He can know joy because you will exude joy in your home, creating a happy environment in which your family can thrive. The woman may be considered the weaker sex physically, but she must live a life of great strength in establishing hope in her home.

While our Father has given us separate and distinct roles to fulfill in our marriages, we must work very hard to live out those roles in unity. There is a great responsibility in pulling your own weight. An unbalanced marriage is like a teeter-totter with both people riding the same end. You really aren't going to go anywhere or accomplish much. If you simply embrace the roles God has given you and live them to the best of your ability, you will build a solid, covenantal, scripturally based marriage that will last.

Next Steps

Questions

Men Only

1. How can I be a better spiritual leader to you?

2. Do you feel I am your protector? Why or why not?

3. If I could do one thing better in my role as your husband, what would it be?

Women Only

1. How can I better submit to your authority in our home?

2. Do I place my identity in Christ or in you?

3. How can I set a better tone in our home?

Activities

1. Read a few books on marriage together.

2. Make a list of the ways you are going to be a better husband or wife. Then set realistic measurements to help you know when you're meeting those goals. For example, "I will lead the family in prayer once a week for the next month." This is a specific and measureable goal that can be modified and improved upon.

three

Gender Differences

In case you didn't know, there are differences between you and your spouse.

When I (Jim) was growing up—with two older brothers and no sisters—I had to take things like soap and shampoo into the shower. When Jerolyn and I got married, there instantly appeared 174 different items in the shower. Now I can't turn around without knocking something over. What are all of these things? I used one of them once, and it made the hair on my back really shiny. Jerolyn has some spongy, poofy thing—I have no idea what it's for and don't really want to know why she needs it.

Jerolyn has often noted that while she gets ready for bed, I go to bed. I brush my teeth and climb into bed, but she has a whole ritual of getting ready for bed, such as washing her face, taking off jewelry, brushing her teeth, taking off makeup, and putting on lotion. For me, getting ready means I brush my teeth and climb into bed. If I do that before she starts getting ready, I am usually fast asleep before she finishes her bedtime ritual.

Unique Attitudes or Perspectives

Beyond such surface differences, men and women also have distinctly different ways of looking at life, love, and their roles in both. Now don't start protesting that this isn't how you and your spouse are. While there are certainly variations and a spectrum of attitudes with both genders, there are also some general perspectives that hold pretty true.

First, men are pursuers, and women like to be pursued. Both genders like the chase, but men typically like to do the chasing, and women like to be chased. Men like to hunt, and women like to be the prize. Men like to conquer and rescue, and women want to be fought for and rescued. Women appreciate the chase, but they want to entice men to pursue them. They want their men to have chivalry and to make every effort to continue trying to win the conquest.

Second, men are fixers, and women are sensors. Men want to solve the problem. Ask a man a question about a relationship, and he will try to fix it. But what women often want instead is for their husbands to just listen intently instead of rushing off to try to fix something. Women are often better at sensing the dynamics within relationship and working through a process to help find a solution.

Third, men are tellers, and women are conversational. There are all sorts of numbers out there on the amount of words men and women use in a day, but for argument's sake, let's go with these: Men use about 25,000 words each day, and women on average use 50,000 or more.[1] Men, save some of your words during the day and share them with your wives at home. Learn to talk with them, and give more than an audible grunt when they ask you a question. As much as I (Jim) like to talk, when Jerolyn asks me how my day went, too often I will say nothing more than, "Good."

Really, that's all? Yes, and it's because so much of the time, I don't consider her desire for conversation and dialogue. I get stuck on seeing things from my perspective, and I get bored listening to me drone on about what happened today. As much as I like to talk, I'm about the bottom line and just want the facts. So that is why it is easy for me to give a short, meaningless answer instead of taking the time to unpack the day. I'm also pretty optimistic, so I will often put the bad stuff out of my brain right away. As soon as it's done, I'm ready to move on and beyond. Later, with all the bad stuff in the past, I can honestly say the day was pretty good for the most part.

But I'm learning that I need to remember to give more details about my day to Jerolyn, to engage in real conversation with her. Honestly, it's good for both of us when I share more. She gets to be more involved in my life, and she is such a great listener and sounding board for me. I like it when we can solve a problem on the spot; so sharing more of my day is a win for both of us. Of course, Jerolyn is also learning that there are still times when "good" is all the response she is going to get that day. And that's OK too, so long as it doesn't remain the default response.

Women, find ways to use up some of your words with others rather than gush them all over your husband. Yes, husbands must learn to listen and share, but be sensitive and avoid saving all your words just for him. Instead, feed him small sound bites, or at least allow him to decompress a bit before trying to engage him in long, deep conversation. You are perceptive and astute; you can see his eyes glazing over in a state of numbness. Rather than become angry, recognize and be sensitive to his "full" meter and show him a little love by slowing down. He probably wants to hear you, just not all at once.

Both husbands and wives must learn to listen and share. And both husbands and wives need to learn and appreciate the differences between men and women and to be sensitive to them so that they can relate to one another caringly and effectively.

Cherish versus Honor

God designed men and women for unique purposes. We each have a job, and when those jobs are done under God's guidance, men and women can work together. In the same way, men and women have unique love languages built into who they are as people. To truly meet the needs of your spouse, you must understand and respect his or her unique perspective on love. This is how God designed us, and while men are different from women and women from men, it's all good.

Several months ago a couple was having some marital conflict. Their problems were not huge, according to them, but significant enough for us to discuss. So I (Jim) suggested that each of them spend some time thinking about and studying a particular word. To the husband, I recommended that he do a word study on the word *cherish*. To the wife, I recommended that she study the word *honor*. These two words are typically included in the vows spoken at most weddings.

Many books have been written about marriage. We have benefited from so many of them. We have learned a lot from William Harley's book *His Needs, Her Needs: Building an Affair Proof Marriage*, which discusses the top needs of both the husband and wife. We also learned from Emerson Eggerichs's book *Love and Respect*, which talks about the love the woman craves and the respect the man wants. Much of what we share in this chapter lines up with these two authors' views on the subject. We believe the words *cherish* and *honor* best describe the highest needs of women and men respectively. Let's unpack this a bit.

Cherish—Speaking Love to Her

When I (Jim) challenged the man to do a word study on *cherish*, I challenged myself to do the same. Here is some of what I learned. To cherish is more than simply to love something or someone; it conveys a deeper way to show love. In Scripture,

Jesus asked Peter three different times if Peter loved him (John 21:15–17). Each time, the Greek word Jesus used for love was different, allowing for a deeper understanding of love than the one English word suggests. That is part of what cherish does for us. Love can be so general and generic, but cherish gives us a better understanding of the commitment and passion we are attempting to express through the word *love*.

Read Ephesians 5:25–29. A husband is to cherish his wife as he would his own body or as Christ does the church. Did you catch that? As Christ does the church. The church is the bride of Christ. How does he love us? He cherishes us. He loves us and cares for us. He lovingly looks on us like a groom looks on his bride. He adores us. That is how a husband is to love his wife: cherishing, adoring, and willing to die for her. A husband who loves his wife is willing to do whatever it takes to protect, care for, and cherish her, just as he would his own body.

Now let's look at the word *nourish* from this same passage. To nourish is to provide that which will best care for and strengthen a person. To nourish your wife is to help her become stronger and healthier so she can strive to be the best she can be in Christ. A husband's job is to build up his wife and support her to become the woman God designed and desires her to be. A husband is to do whatever it takes—no matter what—to nourish his wife just as Christ nourishes his bride, the church. Husband, your words and actions are pivotal in helping your wife see and feel your deep desire to nourish and cherish her. How are you doing?

To cherish something or someone is to hold in high esteem. Imagine holding a precious piece of memorabilia in your hands. It might be an autographed baseball or basketball or a watch given to us by your father. As you hold this prized gift in your hands, you admire, adore, and do all you can to protect it. You almost revere it and show it off whenever you can, but you never let anyone touch it, only look. When I cherish my wife, I adore her, love on her, protect her, and admire her, and let others see her beauty inside and out. All the while, though, I know she is all mine.

For me (Jerolyn), a different word picture comes to mind. To cherish means that my husband covers me no matter what comes in life, whether good or bad, as if he was physically protecting me and preventing the bad from reaching me. I am hidden under his arms, and he hovers over me, not in a condescending or smothering way, but in caring, loving protection.

To love and cherish your bride is to love her unconditionally as much as humanly possible so that she knows that she is secure in your relationship; she can trust you; she knows you are there for the rest of your lives together; any fears that you two would ever be separated are unnecessary. To love and cherish her is to adore her for all she is and all she can become. To cherish her is to celebrate her, love on her, proudly have her as yours, and then be thrilled that she continues to love and have you as her husband. Does she know without question that you love her with all you are? Does she perceive that you cherish her? In what ways can you show her how much you love her? How can you show her that she can trust you and have the security that you two are together for better or worse, in good and bad? Is she assured that you two share a deep, committed love with a vision for the future together, to dream and delight in one another as you grow old together? How will she know as you both grow older that she is still the one for you?

Honor—Speaking Love to Him

Just as women tend to need and want to be cherished, men too have a unique way in which they desire to be loved. A man wants to know that what he does matters to his wife. He wants to hear that his efforts to provide for the family are appreciated by his wife. To devalue what he does devalues him as a person and husband, at least in his perception. What do honor and love have to do with one another? Why does he seem to need respect almost above all else in order to sense genuine love?

In one national study, four hundred men were given a choice between going through two difficult negative experiences. If they were forced to choose one of the following, which would they prefer to endure: to be left alone and unloved in the world, or to feel inadequate and disrespected by everyone? Seventy-four percent of these men said that if they were forced to choose, they would prefer being alone and unloved in the world.[2]

When a wife shows respect for her husband, it speaks volumes to him. When a husband senses respect, he feels supported and encouraged in his role; if it is not present, the marriage seems empty and meaningless to him.

Paul acknowledged the importance of a wife respecting her husband in Ephesians 5: "For this reason a man will leave his father and mother and be united to his wife, and the two will become one flesh. . . . However, each one of you also must love his wife as he loves himself, and the wife must respect her husband" (vv. 31, 33).

In his book *Love and Respect*, Dr. Emerson Eggerichs says it this way:

> Women need to learn how to understand and use the word *respect* because, in truth, respect is a man's deepest value. . . . These men are not saying that they are indifferent to love. They know they need love, but they need to feel respected even more than to feel loved. Perhaps a good analogy is water and food. We need both to survive, but we can live longer without food than without water. For men, love is like food and respect is like water. . . . Respect is the key to motivating a husband.[3]

A few years ago, I (Jerolyn) met one of Jim's mentors. He was a pastor in a thriving church plant and helped Jim navigate the waters of church planting early on. We had only talked briefly after meeting when this mentor looked at me and said, "You don't trust your husband." The statement seemed to come out of nowhere and it made me very angry. My first thought was, "Of course I do." That was quickly followed by, "Who do you think you are? You don't even know me!" Since I completely disagreed with his assessment,

I put his comments aside, justifying my dismissal with the fact that he didn't know what he was talking about. It took me several years to realize, though, that he had been right. He knew I did not trust my husband, not because he had observed it directly, but from his talks with Jim. He could sense from Jim that he was not receiving respect from me in the way he needed to receive it. This mentor saw in my husband's life the negative results of my actions.

To respect someone is to give admiration or honor. To give admiration or honor to your husband is to speak love to him. That is how men are wired to perceive and receive love. They have been designed and called by God to provide for their families and to be the leaders of their marriages and homes. To be recognized for living this out and doing it well is validation of their calling. Just like God instructs men to show love to their wives by cherishing them, God tells wives to honor their husbands because this is how they know they are loved. This is how God designed for men to be loved and for their wives to love them.

A wife gives her husband this honor by loving him for who he is and for his attempts to fulfill his responsibilities to the family. Appreciate and be grateful for his commitment to be respectable. Some men, like me (Jim), are not very handy around the house, but we still attempt to fix what needs repairing or at least find someone else to do it. Wife, do you express appreciation to your husband for what he does to maintain your home? That is one way to show honor and respect, and it speaks volumes to him.

Admiring your husband for the way he treats and loves your family is another form of honor. As your husband attempts to show love by cherishing you, be thankful and express that gratitude to him. Men like that! When your husband expresses love by providing for your family and making decisions based on what is best for all of you, respect and admire him for it. When you fail to express appreciation, and perhaps even express disappointment for what seems undone, it causes a sincere struggle for your husband to remember that he is appreciated and loved. Or, if your husband senses your frustration with his work schedule or that you think he is attempting too much or working too hard, it can cause awkward tension. The reason might be that he is trying to show love for you through providing. Your husband might experience strong tension between wanting to provide yet knowing he needs to be present for you and your family. If he is criticized for not doing enough or for doing too much, he may feel a lack of respect and appreciation or admiration; in other words, he may not feel honored and loved.

Be grateful for your husband's attempts to provide for your family—even if they sometimes seem feeble or like overkill. It shows how much you love him. You honor your husband by appreciating the things he does that are worthy of respect, rather than implying he's not doing enough. All men (and women) are lacking in certain areas; but they also have strengths, and as they gain confidence in how and who God made them to be, they will maximize their strengths. You can help by showing sincere love.

Appreciate and applaud your husband's attempts to be the leader of your home, take care of things, provide and protect, love and cherish you. That is how you honor your husband.

You can also show your husband love by the way you speak about him to others. Proverbs 31 talks about a wife of noble character. It says that her husband is well respected at the place of community leadership. This is partly because she speaks well of and honors him by her words and actions. Husbands earn respect; it is not simply a gift. But it is vital that your husband hears words of appreciation and respect from you—both to him and about him to others. If negative, cutting words are spoken, even in a joking manner, it doesn't feel like respect and love. Be an encourager for your husband. And this goes both ways. Your husband must do the same for you.

Men are designed by God to receive love through honor and respect, but this is not an excuse to ignore the other roles and responsibilities as husband. Men cannot allow work or a career to define them and make the excuse of being so busy "trying to provide" that they ignore their wives' needs in other areas. If you are to be honored, you must earn the right by being honorable. Charles Swindoll, in his book *Strike the Original Match*, said, "It is absolutely imperative, men, that we fight our tendency to be passive in matters pertaining to the home. The passive husband continues to be one of the most common complaints I hear from troubled homes. *Men, get with it!* Your wife will grow in her respect for you as soon as she sees your desire to take the leadership and management of the home."[4] For many years, my (Jim) dad taught me that to earn credibility, I had to be credible. Men, how are you earning credibility at home?

God created us each as unique, complex individuals with different desires and personalities. When you base your marriage on Scripture and work to live your lives pleasing to God and each other, you can learn to celebrate your differences. You do not need to be in competition with each other; instead you can complement one another.

Next Steps

Questions

Men Only

1. When do you feel cherished by me?

2. What could I do better to cherish you?

Women Only

1. Do you feel I talk to you with respect? How can I do better?

2. Do I ever talk disrespectfully about you? Explain.

3. What do I do that makes you feel the most respected?

Activities

1. Take a personality test to learn more about yourself and your spouse. One such test is the DISC Assessment, but there are many to choose from. Discuss (and celebrate) your differences.

2. Talk to one another to discover at least one unique difference between you as husband and wife.

part two

THE VALUES OF
A COVENANT MARRIAGE

four

Define the Seven Values
for Your Marriage

Many people strive to leave an inheritance for future generations but fail to leave a legacy. As parents, for example, we can leave a financial inheritance without the legacy of a good example to guide and direct our children's lives. One of the greatest legacies we can leave our children and others is a godly example in our marriage—a purpose, vision, and plan for a biblical, Christ-centered, covenantal marriage. To leave such a lasting, meaningful legacy—in life or marriage—we need to start with the end in mind.

When my (Jim) mom passed away recently, my family and I noticed that people shared with us—in one or two sentences—what she meant to them. They would say, "She was so wonderful at . . ." or "She cared so much for people." We enjoyed hearing their honest expressions of what her life had meant to others.

What will your tombstone say? What do you want people to remember and say about you when they summarize your life? What kind of legacy do you want to leave? I propose that the greatest legacy is a legacy of faith. Here is how one person briefly summarized his goal in life by visualizing his ideal epitaph: "He was a wonderful husband and loving dad, who was the follower of One, leader of many, and servant of all."

Now, to be more specific, what do you want people to say about your marriage? Every healthy, Christ-honoring marriage is built on shared values. Yet few couples take time to discuss and write out the values for their marriages. As a result, many go through life and marriage without much of a "big picture" or plan.

We understand the need to plan for retirement, though it is said that only a small percentage of people actually do. Instead, they simply hope that funds will be available or that someone will be willing to help take care of them. No planning, just hoping. Such an approach would never fly in business. Corporate leaders organize, cast vision, create values, and put together a business plan. But when it comes to marriage, most of us do not put that kind of intentional effort into creating an overall vision.

But your marriage is worth the effort to do just that; it is worth establishing the core values that will guide your life together. When it comes to marriage, you shouldn't just react and hope it works; you should be proactive and give it the best chance to succeed.

A good place to start is by creating a list of what you both value in marriage. Having a list of shared values helps to avoid confusion regarding what your marriage is about and where it is going. Like in business, you both know what's important and you work together to make it happen.

We have identified and chosen seven key values for our marriage. These are irrefutable, nonnegotiable values that we have decided are what God intends to be the foundation of our marriage. The seven values we have chosen are:

- absolute commitment and unconditional love;
- love God and one another;
- honest communication;
- cherish and respect;
- unwavering support;
- passionate intimacy; and
- playful humor.

You may choose together to adopt these same values, make some minor changes to them, or come up with a completely different way of describing what you both value in marriage. That's fine. Just be sure of two things: that the values you choose are biblically sound, and that you both agree on each value. Two cars on a train will get nowhere if they are pulling in opposite directions. So be prayerful and intentional about making this list.

Absolute Commitment and Unconditional Love

A few years ago, we attended the wedding of some friends. In the ceremony, they chose not to use the usual verbiage of a wedding: for better or worse, till death do us part, and the rest. They simply declared, "I will never divorce you." They were absolutely committed to their marriage and wanted to state their objective and resolve succinctly: This marriage will not end in divorce. Most weddings include vows of commitment, but still about two-fifths of all marriages in America end in divorce. In other words, the vows became empty promises. But this couple was absolutely clear. They vowed not to file for divorce or dissolve their union. They entered into a covenant marriage.

Some may say it is easy to say such a thing at the wedding ceremony and that most people don't go into marriage with plans to divorce. That's true, and they don't. So it begs the question of what happens to those marriages that break up and how the break-ups could have been prevented.

There are few examples in our society today of absolute commitment. In almost every aspect of life, there are choices, and we are usually free to change our minds later. Take, for instance, this computer I (Jerolyn) am typing on. It's a Mac. I've had it for a few years, and I love it. I love that it doesn't get viruses. I love that the operating system is intuitive. I love that the battery lasts for almost four hours. And if anything happened to this computer, I'd get another Mac to replace it. But just a few short years ago, I was a die-hard PC user and had been for twenty years. I was completely sold on the PC product. But obviously, I was not absolutely committed to it. I had some troubles with my PC. It wasn't handling as well as it used to. Tech support was difficult to get. And all my friends and family were using Macs. So when my PC became too sluggish and beat up, I traded it in for a sleeker, new Mac. I had an opportunity to change direction, and I took it.

We could name a hundred and one other areas in life that can be easily traded out on a whim—and that's just in the area of technology. People trade in their old car, get a bigger and better house, and switch jobs. People change stores, restaurants, and churches. And they keep changing because the one they used to like doesn't suit them or meet their needs anymore. We are inundated with the mind-set of "I'm tired of this one; I want to try something else." It's no wonder that this viewpoint has crept into our marriages. Why not? It's so prevalent and seems easy to do.

For many people, trading up to something better has become their default mode and they take the same approach with their spouses. Somehow the "old model" doesn't seem to be keeping up. Surely we can find something sleeker, cleaner, nicer, perkier, and newer. But the one constant in all of these changes is the one doing the trading. Maybe the problem isn't that your spouse and everything else needs upgrading; maybe your heart needs a tune-up or even a complete overhaul.

Divorce is never merely a harmless change; there are always consequences and pain for both spouses and their families. Divorce rips apart two people who had become one life—tied together with family, friends, possessions, memories, and dreams. There is bound to be fallout from such a dramatic separation.

We must alter our way of thinking to guard against the temptation to look at marriage as a temporal, reversible decision. If we approach our marriages with absolute commitment (with not even a thought of leaving our spouses) and unconditional love (no matter what he or she does, I will love him or her), we eliminate the "department store" marriage mentality and focus exclusively on the husband or wife we have chosen for life. Dietrich Bonhoeffer said, "It is not your love that sustains the marriage, but from now on, the marriage that sustains your love."[1]

The wedding and anticipation of living with an amazing person is so overwhelming and exciting that people often forget to contemplate the concept of "forever and always, no matter what." Now is the time—no matter what stage your marriage is in—to choose absolute commitment and unconditional love. Do you find yourself tempted by someone at work? Walk away. Are you frustrated with your spouse's idiosyncrasies? Ignore them. Better yet, look at them as a uniquely endearing part of the person you married. "Never criticize your spouse's faults; if it weren't for them, your mate might have found someone better than you."[2]

One of the greatest helps in choosing unconditional love is to view ourselves realistically. Too often we see ourselves in a rose-colored light and fail to see our faults. When that happens, we see others' faults more glaringly. If we will stop and remember that we're not perfect, and we need grace as much as others do, it's much easier to extend grace to our spouses. We are quick to expect and receive grace. Why is it so difficult to extend that same grace to others? With grace, unconditional love becomes a possibility. If I'm not perfect, and I don't expect my spouse to be perfect, I won't have unwritten conditions on whether I will continue to love him or her. Your spouse does not need to do anything or be a certain way for you to love him or her. You can love because you chose this person to share your life with—blemishes, faults, and all. Whoever your spouse chooses to become, that is who you should love.

Love God and One Another

Absolute commitment and unconditional love are difficult to achieve on our own. There needs to be another factor in the equation—the heavenly Father. When two people are devoted to the Father in every aspect of life, they are able to give the best they are to another person. "A cord of three strands is not quickly broken" (Eccl. 4:12). When God is in the equation, it leads to success in marriage.

One of the greatest obstacles to a lasting marriage is the belief that my needs should be met, and if they aren't, my spouse is not doing his or her job, and I need to find another spouse. That is a lie of the Enemy. Marriage is not a place where another person should meet my needs, but a place for me to meet the needs of another because I have something to give out of my relationship with God. What God is doing in me can be shared with the person to whom I am married. I find my fulfillment in God, not in my spouse. My identity is not in being a spouse, but in being a child of God. My hope is not in my spouse, but in God. My joy is not in a person, but in the divine. Now, that doesn't mean I don't find joy in being with my spouse; I do. But my joy is not dependent on him or her. My joy is in my relationship with the almighty Creator of the universe. And when I take the time to nurture that relationship—with the Almighty—I have an even greater capacity for a powerful relationship with my spouse. I am becoming the person God wants me to be. And even though I haven't arrived yet, I am a person who can love and pour into another to enrich his or her life.

A marriage without God is like two cell phones without chargers. You can communicate for a while—calls, texts, and e-mails. But eventually, if both phones are not plugged in and recharged, they run out of juice. The relationship dies. God is the source of every healthy relationship, because he makes us who we need to be in a relationship. If we are trying to do it on our own, we will run out of juice pretty quickly. We must be plugged into the source.

Honest Communication

Once we have made our choice—an unbreakable choice—and are plugged into the source for our fulfillment and joy, we must devote focused time with our spouses. Bill Doherty said, "If a married couple with children has fifteen minutes of uninterrupted, non-logistical, non-problem-solving talk every day, I would put them in the top 5 [percent] of all married couples. It's an extraordinary achievement."[3] Unfortunately, Bill may not be too far off, and we can't blame it all on our children. Sometimes spouses are just not saving enough intentional words for each other.

We can blame the busyness of life for a large portion of our muteness. We get up early to go to work. Talking is usually an aspect of most jobs throughout the day, and since we think we only have a capacity for a certain number of words each day, many of us believe me have used up our allotment by the end of the workday. We come home tired and spent, thinking of nothing but food, relaxing in front of the TV, hanging with friends, or doing our favorite hobby. The idea of discussing anything more than "The muffler on the car needs to be fixed," or "We have dinner with the Smiths on Friday" can be overwhelming. And some of us hardly even discuss what needs to be done or put on the schedule.

At minimum, we need to commit to having some dialogue again. But the danger with reserving only a few mundane, practical sentences for our spouses at the end of the day is that we stop building a relationship with a loving partner and simply maintain a roommate instead. In a previous chapter, we discussed the use of words and learning to verbally share with each other. But because communication is such a vital part of the marriage relationship, we need to overcome our differences and commit to talking with our spouses.

To continually grow a healthy marriage, the marriage needs to grow deeper, and that can only happen through communicating your heart, desires, hopes, and dreams to one another. If you don't share with each other your thoughts on life, love, politics, religion, and more, you won't know who your spouse is anymore. As you live and grow as human beings, your thoughts and ideas grow and change, too. After you've been married for even ten years, you both are not the same people who walked down the aisle. To stay in a healthy marital partnership, you must share with each other and stay on the same page of life. Otherwise, you'll start to branch off in different directions. Then your spouse will wake up one day and say, "I don't even know who this person is."

Cherish time spent together in conversation. Make it a priority to move past the everyday activities and share your dreams, fears, and hopes. Reaching out to one another in conversation touches the soul and builds a home of commitment.

Cherish and Respect

A man needs respect, and a woman needs to be cherished. We covered this topic in the previous chapter, but this is such an important point that we have chosen to make it a part of our values and celebrate the difference. Ephesians 5:33 says, "However, each one of you also must love his wife as he loves himself, and the wife must respect her husband." This is the way God wired each of us to be. In order to feel any worth in the relationship, the man needs to know that his wife respects who he is and what he does. While he may seem to be the strong, macho superman ready to leap tall buildings and stop speeding trains, he's actually an insecure boy who wants to catch the pretty girl's attention. Much of what he does in providing for and taking care of his wife is his way of asking for approval. He needs to know that his wife trusts him to be all he says he will be. Respect is the very basis of trust. Wife, if your husband doesn't feel that you trust him, he loses confidence in your relationship.

A woman needs to be cherished — placed on a pedestal of honor, loved, and admired as a human being. She wants to be the queen of her home and the most special woman in her husband's eyes. If she doesn't feel this through his actions and words, every other interest her husband has will seem to take her place in his heart. She needs to know that her husband knows her and her needs and that he is willing to go to the ends of the earth to meet them.

There is a little girl in every wife. Husbands, you need to recognize that and do everything you can to show how much you love and adore her. A friend once described it this way: When a daughter is small, she twirls around the room to show off her new dress and get her daddy's approval. She longs for her daddy to cherish her as his daughter. A wife still wants to be cherished and know that the man she married adores her. She will twirl around in a new outfit and ask in a more mature, but still in a "desiring to be loved," way if her husband approves. She asks questions like "Does this dress make me look fat?" "How does this look on me?" and "What do you think of this hairstyle?" Husbands need to recognize that while these questions may seem unimportant compared to the game on TV, their responses are significant to their wives.

If either need—to be cherished or respected—is not being met, the relationship can become distant. When you aren't feeling valued in the way you need, you don't give value back to your spouse.

A large part of cherishing and respecting is to value each other as people. Let your spouse become the individual God designed him or her to be. We are individually and uniquely made. We all have unique talents, gifts, abilities, and personalities. Unfortunately, many people seem to think that being compatible enough to marry someone means the two are essentially the same person. But compatibility does not negate our individuality. We are each designed in a special way to uniquely glorify the Father with our lives. Just because I unite with another human being doesn't mean I stop living out my God-given purpose. The two roles—spouse and individual—can coexist. They are not mutually exclusive.

Actually, we are better spouses when we live out the lives God designed for us. There are times when we have to do jobs or tasks that seem to not be part of who we are. Maybe a spouse has to get the best job available for a time to pay the bills. Because of our responsibilities, we sometimes have to set aside our desires for the greater good. We all have chores at home that are less than meaningful and fulfilling. Does anyone really like to take out the trash? It's just something that must be done. But the final goal should always be to become the best we can be and exactly who God designed us to be. And we should allow our spouses to follow that same journey. Be thankful for the areas of life and interests that you both share, but also celebrate your differences. You are blessed to be married to and sharing life with a uniquely created child of God.

Unwavering Support

Support for each other is part of what it means to be in a partnership. A marriage is not two people walking parallel paths. Instead, it's two people walking the same path arm in arm, heading toward the same goals, running the same race. Each of us is not only looking out for ourselves, but we're watching for the needs of our spouses. We may walk the path in different ways—one may skip while the other jogs. Or we may wear different hats or shoes—one likes Nike while the other likes Adidas. The point is that we're heading in the same direction on the same path and will do everything possible to help the other finish the race with us. For example, the wife might need further education to achieve her professional goals. Therefore, the husband may need to help out financially or pick up some of the duties of the household to free his wife to take the classes she needs. He doesn't do it grumbling or begrudgingly but in complete support of her becoming the very best she can be. When he helps her win, he wins in their partnership as well.

Actions are important in supporting each other, but words can carry just as much weight. We need to be each other's loudest, most boisterous cheerleader. When one wins in some aspect of life, the other applauds. When one stumbles or struggles, the other picks up and helps the partner along. And when one fails, the other gives words of encouragement and solace. Too often we expect more out of our spouses than he or she can reasonably give. With this unrealistic expectation, we tend to put down rather than build up because, in our eyes, our spouses don't achieve what we expect. But if we truly desire to support our spouses, we will offer grace in failures and cheers in accomplishments. *Always* have his or her back in public. We may privately offer constructive criticism to a spouse in a loving way. But in front of others, we must always support our loved one. Bad-mouthing offers no support. It simply tears him or her down in other people's eyes and in our own.

We committed to live our lives with a partner—two becoming one. A major part of that partnership is supporting one another through the good times and the bad.

Passionate Intimacy

Intimacy is an essential component in every marriage and cannot be ignored. The sexual relationship between a husband and wife is one of the most precious gifts the Father has given us to enjoy. It's more than the physical act; it's a spiritual bonding of two people becoming one. Each person's body—the most intimate and personal part of our beings—is given completely to the other for the other's enjoyment. For a woman, sex provides a connection to her husband's heart. She needs that touch and tenderness to feel close to him. That intimacy, can be tied to her basic need to be loved.

A man cherishes intimacy, but he also physically needs the act of sex. A man desires to have sex regularly, and if he doesn't, it can affect him physically and emotionally. Sexual frustration can cause many stresses to surface in a marriage. Those stresses will only fracture the bond, not encourage it.

Nothing can replace intimacy in a marriage. Delighting in one another creates and strengthens a bond that no one can break. It is a precious time for you and your spouse. God designed it, and he wants us to share intimately with one another. We'll say more on this in a later chapter.

Playful Humor

Actress Joanne Woodward said, "Sexiness wears thin after awhile and beauty fades, but to be married to a man who makes you laugh every day, ah, now that is a treat."[4] One of Jim's characteristics that first drew me (Jerolyn) to him was his sense of humor. On our first date, we were in a local ice cream parlor that had a self-serve coffee station. When he got up to fill his coffee, he took the carafe and started moving from table to table filling up everyone's coffee and joking with them. He spread laughter around that little restaurant. Being a more serious person myself, I was attracted to the lighthearted fun in Jim.

We have worked to keep laughter going more than twenty-six years. We love to laugh. There are so many serious topics that we must discuss — our jobs, the children, money, and so on. Taking the time to laugh with one another reminds us that we aren't just partners in life, but that we truly enjoy being with one another. We can look at situations and even ourselves in a humorous way and counter some of the heaviness of life.

Laughing at ourselves is one of the healthiest forms of humility in a relationship. When we see ourselves as fallible humans rather than taking ourselves so seriously, we are so much more pleasant to be around than when we make excuses for our mistakes or place blame on others. When we admit our shortcomings and simply laugh about them, we place ourselves on a common ground with all the other fallible humans. Especially in a marriage relationship, that self-deprecating humor, when done appropriately, clears tension from the air and makes the other spouse feel more accepted, imperfections and all.

So we will continue to laugh at each other and at ourselves, and laugh at our children and at the funny twists in life every day. Laughter will always fill our home.

Although this is not an exhaustive list of values, they are the ones we have chosen to build into our marriage. Maybe you would choose different ones. That is just fine. The marriage trip we will discuss in the next chapter is a great opportunity to hone your list of values for your marriage.

Next Steps

Questions

1. What do you want people to say about you when you are gone?

2. What are "values" to you?

3. What did Christ value?

Activity

1. Research business and church vision statements and value lists.

five

The Marriage Trip

In our first book, *Faith Legacy: Six Values to Shape Your Child's Journey*, we discussed taking a rite of passage trip with your teenager. This is a focused time with your child that includes a mixture of fun and communication. The purpose of the trip is to review the values you have raised them with and to pass the baton. They must begin to take ownership of those values as their own. Planning time away with your spouse to focus on the values in your marriage is just as important.

Some may wonder why it's important to take this trip. Well, that can best be answered by looking at the title of this book: *Faith Legacy for Couples*. Marriages play such a major role in any society. The health of a marriage can shape the entire fabric of a family. If the marriage is struggling, everyone and everything around is affected. Children's lives are disrupted; friendships are damaged; and jobs suffer. But a healthy marriage builds a firm foundation for the family. It forms a sense of security that children need and a hopeful future for the whole family and its community of friends and associates. As believers, we work at our relationships with God. We read his Word, spend time in prayer, gather together for communal worship, and follow the Holy Spirit's leading toward service to others. When something in our lives is of such great importance, we prioritize our time to improve it. Our marriages should be treated in the same manner.

The marriage legacy we leave our children will not only affect their lives as they are growing, but will also influence the relationships they form as adults. With so many attacks on the biblical institution of marriage, we must do everything we can to uphold a standard of excellence. Taking more time to intentionally build our marriage on a foundation of values that will promote growth and harmony is worth the sacrifice of time and money. Marriage is hard work and the more we do to keep it on track and the more safeguards we have in place, the better off we will be. We (Jim and Jerolyn) want to leave to our children — and to those we come in contact with — a legacy of a marriage that is grounded in the Word and based on a set of values that others can emulate. By leaving a marriage legacy based on our faith, we leave a lasting impression far beyond anything we can imagine. Take the time to build a legacy and you and others will see the rewards, now and for generations to come.

On the marriage trip, you and your spouse will be establishing the values for your marriage and begin the work of implementing those values. Maybe you have been married for some time. Consciously or subconsciously, you have been living out a set of values in your marriage. Some are for better and some are for worse. Now is the time to verbalize your values and refocus what you want your marriage to be founded upon. In analyzing the values you have been living by, you may find some problem areas. Most often, problems occur because of living by a poor value or a lack of diligence to live by a good value. Either way, now is the time to straighten out all of the kinks and get back on the right path to a healthy marriage. It is not too late! You just need to intentionally make the right corrections. It's like recalibrating a compass. Over time, the compass can start to slip and fail to give the true direction. By recalibrating it, you get a more accurate reading. It's the same with your marriage. Going through life day-to-day, you might be moving along on autopilot. By doing so, you slowly lose your way, bit-by-bit. The marriage trip is a time to reestablish the right path your marriage needs to take and make sure the instruments guiding you there are true.

Planning a marriage trip is fun and easy; it just takes a little forethought. Begin with your budget and prioritize from there. Here are the elements we see as essential for such a trip:

- a location that is relaxing for both of you—no cell phones, Internet, or TV;

- at least three days focused on your marriage and nothing else; and
- a marriage conference, counseling session, or coaching appointment to participate in.

As you can see, this isn't too complex, but it is intentional. And the simple act of getting away to focus on the values in your marriage will begin to transform your marriage in ways that will last for the rest of your life.

First, carve out vacation days and time away from other responsibilities. Then start working out a budget. The trip can be done on a small or large budget. The point is not where you go (or stay), but that you are together. You can keep it as simple as staying home, sending the kids to the grandparents, turning off all the electronics, and going for walks in the neighborhood. Or you can go as extravagant and exotic as an African safari. The important thing is that you have plenty of focused, uninterrupted time together.

To choose a location, consider a spot that fits both of your personalities. Keep in mind that you want to include some play in this time together. It's not all work. The work will be more productive if you have some fun thrown in as well. For example, Jim loves to golf and fish, and I (Jerolyn) love watching waterfalls and hiking in beautiful meadows and rolling hills. When we are doing those things, we are the most relaxed and disconnected from the duties of life.

Once you have an idea of where you will be, start looking for marriage enrichment opportunities in that area. If you absolutely want to attend a marriage conference, you may need to start with a search on that. You can find many conferences all around the world; by searching the Internet. The dates and locations of the conference you plan to attend will dictate where and when you go on your trip. You can adjust your plans accordingly. The reason we recommend a marriage conference is because it provides a great opportunity to focus your attention on your marriage with some expert guidance and direction. Between the keynote speakers and the breakout sessions, you and your spouse will have an opportunity to explore many topics related to marriage that may reveal trouble areas or reinforce the steps you are already taking. If the time and location for a conference do not coincide with your faith legacy trip, plan on going to a conference together some time in the next year. It will be a great checkup time for how you are doing on implementing the values in your marriage.

Another helpful way to spend your time on your trip is with a marriage counselor or coach. If you've been having some serious problems, a marriage counselor is a must. You and your spouse need to attack your problems head-on before they escalate out of control. However, even marriages that are not facing serious problems can benefit from a counseling checkup with a trained professional. They can affirm you in the areas that you are doing well and help you see areas that could use some tweaking. If not a counselor, consider seeing a coach. Coaches are great for guiding couples through the process of building a healthy marriage. A coach is not one who tells you what to do, but guides you through the process of discovering your own answers to what will make your marriage work. With a Christian coach, you have the added benefit of being guided by someone who uses biblical values as the basis for his or her approach to coaching.

The Vision Statement

Last, but most important, is taking time on your marriage trip to write a vision statement for your marriage listing the values your marriage will be based upon. In the church and business world, many individuals, churches, and companies work hard to create and establish a vision, values, and a mission for their organization but often neglect the critical arena of creating the same for their family life. We want to target the marriage arena to help couples establish and instill a vision, then commit to live out the values that are important to them in having healthy, strong, and more balanced lives and marriages. We are convinced that if people win in their marriages, they will be more productive, better adjusted, and win in other areas of their lives too, including their career. Many of us do a great job of writing business plans for our businesses and checking off items on our to-do lists so we'll be recognized as the best at work, but we neglect this practice in our homes and marriages.

Start by verbally communicating with each other what you see as the preferred future. Part of my (Jim) vision for our marriage is, if God allows, Jerolyn and I will grow old together. If that means we're in wheelchairs across from one another, then I'll hold her hand and let her know she is still the most beautiful woman ever, and I am madly in love with her. You may think that's silly and wonder how it's even a vision. The answer is that it clearly states to her that she is the *only* one for me, and I really do envision us being together for the rest of our lives. It goes to the security and cherishing that we talked about earlier, the things that speak love to her.

After you've brainstormed what the future looks like with the two of you in it together, pare down those thoughts to a simple statement of a covenant marriage commitment you both desire to make and live out. This is a vision or purpose statement for your marriage. The statement that we have chosen for our marriage is: To love, honor, and cherish one another by living out a biblical covenant marriage. The statement is simple, direct, and concise and can be easily memorized. While the wording of the vision statement is not complex, its execution requires intentionality and years of daily hard work.

The Values

Once the vision statement is established, you then decide on those values that you will live out as a couple. There is a direct connection between the vision and values of your marriage. The vision is the big picture, a concise statement from which all else flows in your marriage. The values describe what is most important in your marriage as you pursue that vision.

You don't have to complete everything in one setting, but be purposeful about it. Writing these values may be the hardest thing you do on this trip. It requires focus and honesty, so block out time to work on this list. And remember, nothing is written in stone yet. You may need to do several revisions of your vision statement and values list. That's OK. Take the time to get it right.

One thing to determine when deciding your values is what the absolute, nonnegotiables are in your marriage. These are values that you both agree a healthy, growing marriage cannot live without. That question will help you narrow down to the most important values that you both want in your marriage. And when you disagree, don't be afraid to push back. Discuss these values thoroughly and with open minds.

Don't get hung up on verbiage. Recognize that you each may desire the same value but are stating it two different ways. Keep your eyes on setting your goals, not on the names you give them. Now, be careful here. Two competitive people with strong viewpoints can really butt heads in this process. Keep in mind that you love each other and want your marriage to work. How you get there will probably take compromise on both your parts. But that's OK. If something is so important to your spouse to the point that he or she would state it as a value for your marriage, you should desire to meet that need in his or her life. Just because something isn't important to you doesn't mean it's of no value. As long as your values have a biblical foundation, the possibilities are wide open. Begin by allowing everything to be freely laid out on the table. Then you can start the refining process.

Have fun with the process and have fun with each other. Break up your "work" sessions with playtime. That's why you choose a location you both love and find relaxing. When our son was about four years old, he asked me (Jerolyn) what the word *marry* means. I said, "It's when you spend the rest of your life with your best friend." On this trip, you are with your best friend. Your spouse knows you better than anyone else and loves you more than anyone else. Your happiness makes your spouse happy and vice versa. You are not separate entities choosing opposing goals. Neither are you competitors in the same job. This is a partnership.

This idea of marriage is like a three-legged race. You are tied together. Where one goes, the other must go. So your goals need to be the same. You must move toward those goals at the same pace and in step with one another. What better person to do this with than someone you love with all your heart? Enjoy being with each other and celebrating your amazing life together as a couple.

We have included devotionals in the appendix to begin each day of your trip. They will help start the discussion and get your hearts set on the Father and each other. Do these together so you begin your day on the same page, ready to make your marriage stronger with each step you take in this process.

The marriage trip is only the beginning. We'll talk in the next section about how to implement the values you have chosen for your marriage. That is a lifelong endeavor. After you get home, though, start planning the next time the two of you will get away. It may be only for a night, but put it on the calendar now. You are going to need regular time to enjoy one another, so make it a priority in your schedule now.

The values you established on your trip will not work in your marriage once you are home unless you plan intentional checkup points along the way. To combat complacency, we try to have an annual "state of the marriage" discussion. Like the presidential State of the Union address covers how our country is doing, we celebrate our marital victories and discuss how our marriage is going and where it needs improving. We go out to a nice restaurant and openly talk about how we are doing as a couple. Egos are checked at the door, and we enter into an honest, nonthreatening conversation about our marriage and about met and unmet needs in it. Call it a recalibrating time. You take the time to adjust your clocks that are off by a few minutes. How much more important is it to adjust your marriage back onto a healthy, forward-moving path?

Some changes, small or large, may need to be made to stay on track with the vision for your marriage and to maintain the values you have set. You may choose to revise some of your values, add new ones, or even delete some. Remember that people are moving targets. What was important to you in the past may not carry the same weight today. Determine in your mind beforehand that you will be a willow and not an oak. Oak trees are very stiff and stable. They can't bend. But a willow is flexible and will bend in the wind. For two different people to make a marriage successful, you need to begin with the mind-set of "I'm a willow; I can bend."

Even though you can review your values at the state of the marriage dinner, you need to analyze your progress more than once a year. Assuming that your values will remain firmly rooted and active without maintenance is a recipe for disaster. That's like a football team having a playbook, but never practicing the plays or reviewing execution. It's too easy to get off track, so you want to stay on top of your plan and be sure you are doing what needs to be done to remain healthy. In the back of this book, you will find some questions that will facilitate a discussion of your values. At least once a quarter, sit down and work through those questions to make sure you are both still on the same page in your marriage and plan.

King David said, "I have hidden your word in my heart that I might not sin against you" (Ps. 119:11). In following that same principle, we encourage you to print out your values on nice stationery and hang them on the wall. Use something that is not permanent to hang them, because you'll want to move them around periodically. Like anything, we become accustomed to seeing something in one place over and over and then end up not seeing it at all. To keep your values fresh in your minds, move them around the house so that you are constantly aware of them. Get some dry erase markers and write one value a week on your bathroom mirror as a reminder. Or put a post-it note on your computer or in your lunch sack. Use your imagination. The point is to creatively keep your values always before you and on your minds. Your marriage is too important to take a trip and then let everything you did die away. Keep moving forward together, united and with purpose.

Next Steps

Questions

1. Where is one place we would both love to go together in the next six months?

2. What is the number one goal for our marriage?

3. What are the irrefutable, nonnegotiable things we value in our marriage?

4. How does the answer to question 2 above fit into a values list?

Activities

1. Plan a Faith Legacy Trip.
2. Write a vision statement.
3. Write out the values for your marriage.
4. See a marriage counselor or coach.
5. Attend a marriage conference.

part three

STRATEGIES FOR BUILDING YOUR MARRIAGE

six

Strategy 1: Devotion to God

Many people believe in the values it takes to have a good marriage such as trust, honesty, love, and patience. They know that the health of a marriage in great part depends on being loyal to these values. Even most people who do not believe in God know these are good values to have in a marriage. But by focusing only on the values, they have missed one element of the equation. To be able to fully live out these values and maintain a healthy, vibrant, growing marriage relationship, you must die to self.

As believers, the basis of our relationships with God is a surrender of our wills, which are carnal desires, to the will of the Father, which is righteousness. When we take that step of faith, we no longer live to accomplish our own plans, but to fulfill what the Father has for our lives. We surrender our selfishness to become the people he designed us to be, and we trust in his all-sufficiency. Larry Crabb said it like this: "And all we need to live as Christians, no matter what our circumstances, is the security of [God's] love and the significance of participation in [his] purpose. We must never claim that our relationships with others do not affect us deeply: they do. But Christ's resources are enough to keep us going."[1] He is our all in all. As his children, we have given up our rights and place our trust in him—desiring to live out our lives for him.

When we enter into a marriage relationship, we are striving for a similar relationship. Crabb further says, "Upon reckoning what is true—that I am secure and significant in Christ—I must by faith approach my wife as a personally full husband, willing to share the love shed abroad in my heart, needing nothing in return."[2] We no longer live for ourselves. We have another person to consider. Thus, goals for my life are not set with only me in mind. They are set to help me become the kind of person who can faithfully love, honor, and cherish my spouse. The biggest problem that arises in striving for these goals when God is left out of the equation is selfishness.

All sin begins with selfishness. I steal to get more for myself. I lie to make myself look better or to get away with a wrong I have done. I cheat to advance myself more quickly or to satisfy my desires without earning the rewards. I sin in my anger because I don't get my way. I covet because I want something that someone else has. Selfishness robs us of any hope of surrendering ourselves fully to another person, because all of our attention is focused on what we want without consideration for anyone else. As humans, we tend to be very selfish. In most situations, the first thought is "How will this affect me?" or "What will I get out of this?" In marriage, as in all of life, this is a recipe for disaster. After getting married, your thinking must always take into consideration, "How will this affect my spouse?" or "What will my spouse get out of this?"

Peggy Noonan, columnist for *The Wall Street Journal*, told a story that provides an incredible image of selflessness in her article, "Welcome Back, Duke."

Once about 10 years ago there was a story — you might have read it in your local tabloid, or a supermarket tabloid like the National Enquirer — about an American man and woman who were on their honeymoon in Australia or New Zealand. They were swimming in the ocean, the water chest-high. From nowhere came a shark. The shark went straight for the woman, opened its jaws. Do you know what the man did? He punched the shark in the head. He punched it and punched it again. He did not do brilliant commentary on the shark, he did not share his sensitive feelings about the shark, he did not make wry observations about the shark, he punched the shark in the head. So the shark let go of his wife and went straight for him. And it killed him. The wife survived to tell the story of what her husband had done. He had tried to deck the shark. I told my friends: That's what a wonderful man is, a man who will try to deck the shark.[3]

When push came to shove, this husband had no thought for his own safety, but only for the well-being of his wife. We need to be freed from our self-centered thinking so we can focus on the needs of our spouses. We must grow in our individual relationships with God and let him transform us into people who can give completely to our spouses. We should want to be the people who will deck the shark for our spouses.

Scripture

Once the decision to follow Christ is made, it's time to become who God designed you to be. It takes a commitment of time, and it begins in his Word. Everything you need for a healthy life and marriage is found in the Word of God if you study and apply it to your life. As we have said, success in marriage begins when we surrender to Scripture. James addressed the power of the spoken word and how it can build up or destroy (3:1–12). Paul talked about perfect love in 1 Corinthians 13—a love that Christ demonstrated and that we must always strive to achieve. Paul also gave invaluable relational instruction in Ephesians 5. James taught about anger and the ways to deal with it without harming a relationship (1:19–20). And finally, Christ's parables, not to mention his life, contain many examples of the power of selflessness. You will grow up when you apply these lessons and, in the process, you will strengthen your marriage relationship.

The spiritual journey is a personal one, but it is designed to be accomplished in community. The most intimate partnership on that journey is with your spouse. Spend time reading God's Word together and discussing its meaning, intrinsically, as well as for your lives as individuals and a couple. Attend a Bible study together. Post Scripture around your home to remind you of his promises and directives. Make the Word of God the basis of your decisions and the judge of your disputes. God's Word was relevant when it was written, and it is relevant today. Learn and grow from its wisdom and your marriage will be the stronger for it.

Prayer

The Word of God is the instruction book, but prayer is the power. Simply reading Scripture does not change us; we must first communicate with the Father regarding his Word. Prayer is an open communication with the Almighty. It's two-way, 24/7 access to the one who loves us unconditionally and wants the very best for our lives. It's the general's communiqué with his soldier and the patient's call to his counselor. Prayer is curling up in our daddy's lap with his protective arms wrapped around his child. As you build a relationship with your spouse, you need to talk with the perfect one to know how to deal with a marriage formed by two very imperfect people.

Think about it. Marriage involves two fallible, sinful humans living together in a corrupt world full of temptations and troubles. Such conditions are like locking two sugar addicts in a candy factory. But with continuous access to the Almighty, you have the power to deal with, first, your own imperfections, then your spouse's, and then the rest of the world. You can cry out to God in pain, or you can laugh, dance, and sing his praises. You can seek his guidance on a difficult frustration with your spouse, and you can offer thanksgiving to him for blessing you with a helpmate. You don't have to struggle in your imperfection, wrestling with a fallible spouse. You can take your cares to the Father. The greatest gift you can give your spouse is to lift him or her up to the Lord in prayer. In those moments, you surround your spouse with the power of the Almighty. And as a couple, you can seek the Lord's direction together in every matter you face. You join together to work toward one mission, accomplishing the will of the Father. In prayer you, as a couple, rise above your imperfection and become perfect in him. It's in that attitude that anything is possible. Hurts will be healed. Misunderstandings can be cleared up. Decisions will be made. Joy can return to your relationship.

Worship

And in that attitude of joined prayer, we can worship our Lord together—with combined hearts honoring one Lord. Personal and corporate worship are vital elements of a healthy relationship with the Father and other believers. Many believe that if they attend church once a week for the music portion, then they have worshiped. But they are missing the complete picture. Worship is more than music. It involves standing before the Lord uninterrupted, free from distractions, focused completely on him. It includes studying his Word and meditating on it; it involves prayer—speaking, and more importantly, listening. But some expression of praise is needed in the worship experience, as well. Music, art, poetry, dance—these are amazing tools for worship. There is something about the arts that touches our souls in a special way. Art and music reveal a bit of God's heart and give us a glimpse of heaven. Few events in life cause us to stand in awe, but the beauty of the arts can. And we have the privilege of using these arts to worship our God, and they please him. We don't have to be a professional artist or even a proficient one. He hears and sees our hearts' expression.

A few years ago, I (Jerolyn) was on a worship team at a youth convention. There were twelve worship leaders plus the main leader each on a microphone, a full band, and about twelve hundred teenagers in a ballroom all lifting their praises to God. It was loud, energetic, and beautiful. At the end of one song, we were so caught up in praise and the presence of the Holy Spirit that we stopped singing the words to the song and simply lifted praises to God. "Hallelujah," "I love you," and "We praise you, Lord" rang around the room. In that moment of praise, my ears suddenly focused on my own voice. Now I'm not one who has any illusions of grandeur about my singing voice. It's passable. But in that moment, it was the most beautiful voice I had ever heard. I remember thinking, "Lord, this can't be my voice. It is so beautiful." I've never heard God speak audibly to me, but this is one of the times I came the closest. He clearly spoke into my heart these words: "This is what I hear when you sing my praises."

I learned a very valuable lesson that day. The level of talent doesn't matter; what counts is the heart. The Lord desires for you to sing, dance, play an instrument, or draw praises for him in any manner you want, with all your imperfections, as long as your heart is reaching out to honor him. Lift up your offering to him.

Worship him in your alone time, in corporate worship with other believers, and most importantly with your spouse. We have seen couples, who prefer different worship styles, start attending different churches. But they lack the spiritual connection in their relationship. I (Jerolyn) have experienced a powerful connection to Jim in moments when we are standing with arms raised praising our Father together—a connection unlike any I have with anyone else in the room. If he is not beside me, I am missing out on one of the spiritual connections of our marriage. But it is not only the music. Listening to the same sermon provides us a common ground from which we can discuss the Word and grow together in its message. Marriage is a uniting of two people to become one, and worshiping together is one of those areas in which we need to remain united.

Service

Scripture, prayer, and worship are the first three bases of building a healthy relationship with the Father. The fourth is service. Service is the giving of your time and talents to the furthering of God's kingdom. It can be as small as opening the door for a stranger in need to taking a mission trip to Africa. We can engage in acts of service every day. Jesus said, "I tell you the truth, anyone who gives you a cup of water in my name because you belong to Christ will certainly not lose his reward" (Mark 9:41). Our eyes should be constantly looking for those opportunities and our ears attentive to the Holy Spirit's prompting us to do them.

You and your spouse may have very different talents that lead you to serve in different ways. For example, one of you may work well with children, while the other one works well with his or her hands. There are places for both kinds of talent in- and outside the church setting. However, there are also many opportunities to work together as a couple serving others. Most churches have service projects. Our church, The River, gives a community Christmas party as a gift to some people who are struggling economically. Many couples work together to make that morning special for those who may not otherwise have a Christmas. They serve breakfast, provide crafts, or assemble bicycles to give to the children. There is joy that comes from serving. By serving others with your spouse, you have an opportunity to share a special and unique time together.

Shared experiences are a human joy we all love to have. Recently, I (Jim) had the privilege of being with our daughter and her fast-pitch softball team while they played in a tournament in Colorado. Jerolyn was unable to come with us. As I watched the girls play their hearts out, I acutely missed Jerolyn's presence beside me. Here was a moment of such joy for our daughter and her team, yet the closest I could come to experiencing it with Jerolyn was through texts. Serving together is an example of the kind of shared experience that I longed for during that fast-pitch softball game.

Finding a place of service is the most important place for a Christian to be. We are not only following God's directive to serve others, but in serving we will find our greatest joy. And sharing that with your spouse makes the work extra special and strengthens the spiritual bond between you.

A Day Alone with God

Both of us (Jim and Jerolyn) at times take a Day Alone with God (DAWG). It's an important part of our growth as believers. We get away from the usual work schedules and busyness. With just our Bibles in hand, we spend time focusing on the Father and what he has to say to us.

For years we did this separately and still do. But we have also found that occasionally we enjoy taking the time away together. We had an opportunity to get away to a hotel for a couple of nights. So we decided to make it days away with God. We read Scripture together, listened to worship music, prayed together, and even sat in silence together. Sometimes we did things separately, but for the most part, we had two days of worshiping our Lord together. It was a very precious time for us. While at first it may have been a little awkward, we soon accepted our spiritual vulnerability and engaged fully in the experience. Whether you take your days alone with God apart or together, it will have an invaluable impact on your relationship with the Father and with each other.

Living out the Christian life and building a marriage are two important and yet time-intensive tasks. But if you take the time to focus on the former, it will spill over into the latter. Your marriage cannot do anything but grow and benefit from a closer walk with the Lord. He designed the sacrament of marriage and desires to be smack dab in the middle of yours. Invite him into your marriage and let him grow you together like never before.

Next Steps

Questions

1. Ask yourself: How can I better my spiritual health?

2. How can I help you grow spiritually?

3. What would you like me to hold you accountable to doing or being in your spiritual walk?

Activities

1. Go to church together.

2. Join a small group together.

3. Go on a mission trip together.

4. If you don't already do so, pray together.

5. If you don't already, read the Word together and/or do a Bible study.

Strategy 2: Dialogue

Today's communication technology has absolutely exploded. We have e-mail, cell phones, text messages, instant messaging, Skype, Twitter, and Facebook, along with good ol' snail mail. Yet in this age of instant contact, with the ability to know what someone is doing and where they are doing it virtually every moment of the day, many marriages are still sorely lacking in communication. Now we (Jim and Jerolyn) are not techno haters; we use all the latest gadgetry. But technology has not enhanced communication as much as we would like to think. Instead it has often replaced the sit-down, face-to-face conversations that are desperately needed. Our communication skills have been reduced to short, misspelled snippets of timely information.

We have lost the art of dialogue. Do we still know how to express ourselves using adjectives, words longer than five letters, and complete sentences? Can we still have a good and fair debate? Is it possible for us to listen not only to someone's words, but to his or her heart? These are practices that married couples seem to be engaging in less often. We have too many other distractions at our disposal. When planning a date, it is much easier to go pay twenty dollars and sit together quietly in front of a movie screen than to fix a meal and have a meaningful conversation. But which one is going to build your relationship with your spouse? Not to say that an occasional movie is wrong. The point is that you need to spend more time as a couple talking—sharing your dreams, fears, hopes, and desires. You need to plan together for your future and the future of your children. One of the best things we did at the beginning of our relationship was to choose not to go to movies. Instead, we spent time talking over a cup of coffee or a meal. When you open up the communication lines, you open up an exponential growth opportunity for your marriage.

We have broken the topic of dialogue into four sections—basic life communication, facing conflict, heart-sharing, and dreaming together. Each area of communication needs your time and management to build a relationship. Knowing how to do them well takes time and practice.

Basic Life Communication

All marriages share the need for communication about basic life needs. We must discuss who is cooking dinner and paying the mortgage. We need to know each other's schedules for the week to plan who needs to get where at what time. We call this mundane or life-specific communication. These discussions are important in marriages and many other types of relationships as well. Roommates, for example, need to have mundane, life-specific discussions. If the toilet is clogged, who is going to call the plumber or the superintendent? If the trash needs to go out, who is going to be sure it happens? Life-specific conversations may not be the most interesting ones to have, but they are necessary for a household to function smoothly. We simply must have these conversations to stay in touch with those areas of our lives that need to be managed.

One approach to strengthening this type of communication is to start with an overview conversation on Sunday night followed by morning reviews each day. Discuss schedules for the week and work out the logistics that need to be covered. Be sure you have an understanding of mealtimes, including who will be there and who will cook. Work out carpools and shopping needs. Working out this plan together ensures that everything will get done and no assumptions will be made. Verbalized expectations save a lot of frustration.

After life-specific conversations come life-general discussions. These dialogues have nothing to do with schedules or chores. They are a time to have one-on-one, face-to-face talks about life. Share your philosophies on life with each other. They can be as broad as what fears you have right now or how you feel about the present administration in the government. Maybe you need to discuss your views of God or haggle over a passage of Scripture. Talk about current events in the world and what they could mean for the future of a particular country and its people or for the future of the world. These don't have to be long, heavy, drawn-out dialogues. But they do need to happen regularly. One of our favorite regular discussions starts with asking each other these questions: "What has the Spirit been impressing on you lately?" or "What is God teaching you?" With these questions, we can measure how we each are doing spiritually, and also learn how to pray for each other.

By asking your spouse's opinion about various ideas and happenings in the world, you grow to know each other better. Many times, we might fear how our spouses will react to a particular situation simply because we've never discussed such things happening. We have no idea what their reactions will be. But if we've discussed similar occurrences in the world, then we know their takes on those situations and thus have no reason to wonder how they will react. It's one thing to know your spouse's favorite color or food, but when you get to know the way he or she thinks and processes life, you are truly learning who he or she is at the deepest level.

A third area of communication that must occur between couples is in the area of finances. The number one disagreement within a marriage is due to finances. It can range from "We don't have enough money" to "We have too much money." Finances can be tricky to navigate. But it can be done with open communication, humility, and honesty. Begin by identifying and admitting to how you each manage money. Often a marriage will include one spender and one saver. Or maybe you are both savers or spenders. Once you have honestly looked at how each of you think about finances and what your tendencies are, you can set up your finances in a way that doesn't indulge either party. Build a plan you can agree on, and don't forget to enjoy working together. You are engaging in a shared challenge—make it fun. Set goals and celebrate them when they are reached. View your finances as an ongoing project you continually work on together. If you face them together with honesty, your finances won't be a marriage difficulty.

Another area that requires effective communication is parenting. If you don't currently have children and don't plan on having children, feel free to skip ahead. But if you have children or hope to one day, this is definitely worth addressing. Parents must be on the same page when it comes to disciplining, directing, and modeling for your children the life and values you want them to learn. We (Jim and Jerolyn) are convinced that having a godly, covenantal marriage is one of the best ways of showing our kids how to live and love one another till death do us part. One of the best examples I (Jim) can show to our children is loving and cherishing their mom. I want our girls to know that a woman is to be loved unconditionally by her husband and that their mom means more to me than any other person on this earth. I want our girls to see this modeled and expect it from whom they choose to marry. I want our son to see how a man should adore and cherish his wife. I want him to have a legacy of loving his wife the way God intended and to learn well from his dad.

We want our kids to see us show affection and demonstrate our love for one another. Your children may think it is awkward or weird to see their parents show affection, but they appreciate later the love and tenderness they see their parents express. Gabby, our youngest, has always tried to squeeze in the middle of us to push us apart when we were hugging or kissing in the kitchen. Even today, at seventeen, Gabby still pushes between us when we kiss. It has now almost become a fun little game with Gabby to make us laugh and remind us of our "little girl."

Couples who have not discussed how to parent together will experience a lot of frustration—and so will their children. Avoid the heartache, and figure out a plan ahead of time. There are many great parenting books, but, of course, we recommend that you read our book, *Faith Legacy: Six Values to Shape Your Child's Journey* (Indianapolis: Wesleyan Publishing House, 2009). *Faith Legacy* will help you create a plan for parenting. Everyone will know the expectations and work toward the same goals. But don't just set goals and stop with that. You as parenting partners must continue to communicate with each other about your children and their upbringing. Although your basic value system remains the same, how you instill those values may change from child to child. Each child is a unique individual. Respect the person each child is by taking the time to disciple him or her to be the person God designed him or her to be.

Facing Conflict

Now that we have laid out some basic areas of communication that need to happen between a husband and wife, we want to discuss some principles of dialoguing together in certain types of situations. The first is learning how to handle conflict. We face conflict almost every day. When you live in a world of imperfect people with prideful hearts, there will be conflict. We have to learn to deal with conflict in our jobs, government, communities, and homes. As much as we may hate to confront conflict, it is inevitable.

Most principles of conflict management apply across the board, but there is an additional facet of marital conflict that makes it just a little bit different from other kinds of conflict. In the workplace or the community, for example, we can easily find the time and space to distance ourselves a little from the situation to regain perspective. But when we are dealing with our spouses—the people we love the most in the world and with whom we are closest—it can be difficult to find the space to regain the perspective we need to resolve the conflict. Here are some key things we (Jim and Jerolyn) have learned about handling conflict in marriage.

First, do not live under the delusion that you will never have conflict. In the early stages of a marriage, everything may be ooey-gooey, lovey-dovey perfect, and you might have little or no conflict at all. But as time goes on, you settle into your married life and routines; you continue to grow as an individual; and your love moves to a deeper level. Inevitably, you will hide less and become more open with your opinions. As this happens, you may learn that you and your spouse differ in your opinions on some pretty key areas. What do you do with those differences?

Too often married couples take one of two paths. One is to avoid conflict by stuffing down opinions and refusing to say anything. The intention is just to get along and keep peace. However, the peace is only external and probably only for a time. Those stuffed feelings are eventually going to come out at some point and perhaps cause an even bigger conflict than the initial problem warranted. It's like lava building up inside a volcano— eventually it is going to erupt.

The second path is to hold nothing back, spewing every opinion without regard for the thoughts and feelings of the other person. No thought is given for the other person's emotional well-being and no respect for his or her opinion. Kindness is not even a consideration. The only goal is to forcefully make feelings known, without any care for what is being done to the other person.

Both pathways have a problem. The first one—avoidance of conflict—is based on fear. When you stuff down a problem and ignore it, it's often because you fear one or more of the following: (1) offending the other person, (2) having your ideas put down,

(3) starting an argument, or (4) making your spouse angry. But by avoiding conflict and refusing to discuss the disagreement, you feed the fear. But fear is not the place to allow your marriage to reside. By allowing fear to win, you avoid dealing with issues that need to be dealt with. Not only are those issues left unresolved, but they will drive you to frustration, which will in turn lead to resentment.

When resentment comes, it drives a wedge into every aspect of your marriage and separates you spiritually and sometimes even physically. This separation usually takes place over time and sneaks up on many marriages. It's a lot like the proverbial frog in the kettle. It is said that if you place a frog into a pot of boiling water, he will immediately jump out. But if you put the same frog into a pot of cold water and slowly heat it up, the frog will not notice the change in temperature and will slowly boil to death. Avoiding conflict will do something similar to your marriage. When you are afraid to face your conflicts, resentment slowly creeps into your life until you reach a boiling point in your marriage. Allowing fear to control you and your marriage will destroy what was once precious to you. You can't let fear have that kind of hold on your family.

While the route of fear and conflict avoidance can destroy a marriage, the other pathway is just as devastating. To simply spew opinions with no thought for the other person's feelings is a sign of arrogance. It seems to start innocently enough, almost in a joking manner. Without even realizing it, you can easily fall into a habit of belittling your spouse through your words, actions, and attitudes. But then when you have a disagreement, the "innocent" belittling quickly turns into disrespect, unkindness, and a basic lack of love. In your arrogance and feeling of superiority, you might even say things to your spouse that, because of basic courtesy, you would never say to another human being. Yet you are somehow unable to extend that courtesy to your own spouse—the one you have chosen to love and do life with—because it has become a habit to belittle.

Pride is a powerful emotion. It can challenge even our basic values. Many people lie to avoid exposing weaknesses. That is because of pride. And it is in our pride that we view our opinions as right and all others as wrong. When we enter into a conflict with that attitude, there is no resolution possible except to break the will of the other person. That isn't to say that we never enter into a conflict with the right answers. We may be absolutely right. But if the attitude of our hearts is arrogance, we may still end up in the wrong. Jesus said, "Blessed are the peacemakers, for they will be called sons of God" (Matt. 5:9). As believers, our conflict resolution must be based on Scripture. Success in marriage happens when we surrender to Scripture.

Learning how to fight fairly takes forethought and humility. You need to speak not out of anger or hurt, but with a thoughtful perspective of the situation. Take some time to review what the conflict is:

- How important is it?
- Do I have the right attitude?
- Am I taking things too personally?
- What point do I really need to get across?
- How do I make my point without hurting my spouse?

Once you've worked out your own issues over the situation and have your argument in line, you need to walk into the discussion with humility. A great starting point is to have an understanding that your way is not always the right way or the only way to look at a problem. When one of us is so competitive and insecure that we always have to be right and win, we lose as a couple. One of the word pictures we have attempted to use — even in our disagreements, arguments, and fights — is that we are both tugging on the same side of the rope. I (Jim) want Jerolyn to know that I am willing to die for her, and she is worth the fight to win her love and trust. Yes, there are times, unfortunately, that the fight turns into me just trying to win. The fight turns into a fight, and we lose sight of what really matters — resolving the issue at hand and doing our best to objectively debate the issue and not each other. When we are confident that we are both pulling on the same side of the rope, we realize we are not fighting against one another, but rather, fighting *for* one another and our marriage. So why do we want to win so badly? What is it in us that wants so badly to be right that we are willing to damage the relationship? What would happen if we honestly laid our egos and insecurities off to the side and cared for one another when disagreeing?

We have one friend who tells couples that it is OK to fight; but before they fight, they have to stop and pray with each other. It's amazing how hard it is to be mad at the one to whom you just expressed your love through prayer.

It's OK to not always be right. Beginning with a humble heart will soften your whole demeanor as you approach a dialogue with your spouse. You will be more rational and kind when you face conflict with a prepared heart. You can't always control how your spouse will respond, but you can control yourself.

Heart-Sharing

While moments of conflict are inevitably going to occur in every marriage, hopefully you'll have many more times of heart-sharing. What is that? It's saving some words for each other at the end of the day to simply connect and see how the other *really* is doing. Ask about each other's day and then answer with more than "Fine." Tell each other about your highs and lows, what was good about your day and what was challenging. Seek each other's counsel on problems. Share lessons you learned and how you are striving to do better in various areas of your life. Be open and honest with your joys, fears, frustrations, and hopes for your job, marriage, and kids.

Allow your spouse to enter into your day and be a part of it. You may not know much about the specifics of doing each other's job, but you understand deadlines, conflict management, calendars, goal setting, relationship building—all the aspects that are involved in every job. Those are the parts you can share together so you know what each other's day-to-day life is like. Have an insatiable curiosity regarding every aspect of your spouse's day. Not in a creepy sort of stalking way, but in a loving way of saying, "I care about what you did today and how you did in it."

Heart-sharing may be tough for some because you are tired at the end of the day. If your job involves a lot of talking, you may be talked out. But look at this time as an investment. You are putting time into the most important relationship in your life, second only to God. You are showing love and care in a tangible way by caring about how your best friend lives life when you are not there and sharing your day with your spouse. Take the time. It's worth it.

Dreaming Together

Finally, dream together. Dreams are important. When you stop dreaming, you stop moving forward, and life becomes just a management position. You do the same thing over and over again without change or progress. But when you dream, you see new possibilities, and growth can happen.

Since we (Jim and Jerolyn) are in the ministry, we tend to dream a lot about the ministry. We can spend a lot of time coming up with ideas and dreams for the church, books, conferences, and coaching opportunities. That's not a tough one for us.

It seems to flow naturally, because we work together and are passionate about it. You may not be in career ministry, but maybe you do volunteer work or another kind of project together. Dream about the possibilities for that ministry or project together. Brainstorm ways to improve it or take it a different direction to reach more people. If you have separate careers, dream with each other about your careers. Do you have kids? You can always dream about ways to improve your relationships with your kids and dream about the future with them. We are always talking about what life will be like when our kids are all grown and married. For example, we want to take family vacations together at least every other year. We dream about the different places we want to go and what we will do there together.

One of the things we love to dream about together is our marriage. What do we dream about for our future? What dreams and desires do we have for us? What places or goals do we pray that God will allow us to share together? What kind of "bucket list" do you have for things that you would like to experience together someday? Dream about what your marriage will become as God allows you to live many more years together. Pray that God will show you his dreams for you so that you can experience the reality of your God-given dreams coming true in your marriage. With God, there is no ceiling. Dream big within God's vision for your lives together.

Dream about everything—job promotions or options, vacations you want to take, people you want to spend time with, places you want to visit, books you want read, people you want to meet. The list is endless if you let yourselves go. Dreams are free and bountiful. Who knows how God might make one of your dreams come true. Sit down, pick a topic, and start dreaming together. You may be amazed at the ideas that flow, and how one day you will be able to remember that you were blessed to do it together.

Next Steps

Questions

1. Do I save enough words for you at the end of the day?

2. How can I better listen to what you have to say?

3. What can I do to handle conflict between us better?

4. Tell me your dreams—for yourself and our marriage.

Activities

1. Go over your finances together.

2. Plan at least thirty minutes of face-time a day where you can talk openly.

3. Take walks or go to a favorite restaurant for dessert or coffee to allow for talking and sharing.

4. Discuss current events.

5. Plan how you will fight fairly next time you disagree.

eight

Strategy 3: Demonstrate

Gary Chapman wrote a wonderful book called *The 5 Love Languages: The Secret to Love That Lasts.*[1] In it, he describes the way people give and receive love. By really knowing your spouse, you can show him or her your love in the language that he or she will receive it best. If your husband is a gift giver, then giving him a gift will show your love. If your wife's love language is acts of service, then show her your love through doing things such as emptying the dishwasher without being asked or taking out the trash. The feelings of love are important. The commitment of love is vital. And the act of love is irreplaceable. We can say all day long that we love each other, but unless we show that love with our actions, the words are empty. It follows the old adage, "Actions speak louder than words." And in a marriage, your actions either scream, "I really don't care about you" or they say, "You mean the world to me, and I would do anything for you."

Speaking love is fine, but living it out can be really tough. Intentional actions of love require thought and selflessness. There is a story about a church in Minnesota that had a marriage seminar for husbands. At one session, the pastor asked a man who was approaching his fiftieth wedding anniversary, Ole Westrum, to share the secret to staying married to the same woman for so many years.

"Vell," Ole replied, "I've tried to treat her nice, spend da money on her, but best of all, I took her to Norvay for da twentieth anniversary!"

The pastor responded, "Ole, you are an amazing inspiration to all the husbands here! What are you planning for your fiftieth anniversary?"

Ole proudly replied, "I'm a-gonna go back to get her."

OK, so maybe that is not the best example of showing love. This chapter, however, describes a few kinds of realistic, active love moments to get you thinking of ways to pour love into your spouse's life.

Meet Needs

Ask what your spouse's needs are and then meet them. When we (Jim and Jerolyn) have our annual state of the marriage discussion, one of the main questions we ask is: "How can I meet your needs better?" Serving one another takes a servant's heart. Jesus demonstrated this for us in John 13 when he washed the disciples' feet. Wearing sandals in an arid, sandy country made for some dirty feet. When a guest came into the house, a servant washed the guest's feet and made the guest feel welcome. In the same way, Jesus humbled himself and served the disciples with a beautiful act of love by washing their feet. The prince of the universe bowed to the needs of those he created. How much more should we meet the needs of our spouses! And why don't we? The top reasons are probably laziness, selfishness, and pride. And worse yet is not taking the time to figure out what our spouses' needs are—whether by observation or simply by asking them what they need from us.

One roadblock may be your obstinacy. If you don't think your needs are being met, you may not value taking the time to meet your spouse's needs. I (Jim) remember when I was doing a study about loving my wife. It was something I already knew, but for some reason, the realization had never clicked. When I quit focusing on myself and began to genuinely attempt to meet her needs, it's amazing how so many of my needs were met. Yes, I am like most men—a little thick in the skull and a slow learner. But this idea revolutionized the way I looked at and treated my bride. I believe my obedience in this one area changed our marriage from something that was good to something that became great.

How often do we as husbands or wives expect our spouses to meet our needs? How often do we even share what those needs are rather than expecting the other to figure it out? "Well, if I have to tell you, then you just don't care." We often attribute this to women, but men are just as guilty. We expect our spouses to know before we know ourselves, or we become so selfish and inwardly focused that we expect others to respond to our needs without any warning or request, except maybe an outburst of "What about me?" or "Why don't you care for me?"

There is a beautiful phenomenon regarding acts of love. When you work to meet your spouse's needs, you will find that he or she will work harder to meet your needs. It's the reciprocity of love. When your spouse does something nice for you, because you love him or her, you want to return the love by doing something nice in turn.

Listen

A second way to demonstrate love is by listening. Not hearing, listening. They are two very different actions. You may hear your spouse say, "Are you going to be late coming home again?" But if you listen, he or she is probably saying, "You've been working a lot lately, and I miss you. I really need more time with you."

The story goes that a man asked his wife, "What would you most like for your birthday?"

"I'd love to be ten again," she replied.

On the morning of her birthday, he got her up bright and early and off they went to a local theme park.

What a day! He put her on every ride in the park: the Death Slide, the Screaming Loop, the Wall of Fear—everything there was! Five hours later she staggered out of the theme park, her head reeling and her stomach upside-down.

Right to a fast food restaurant they went, where her husband ordered her a big burger with extra fries and a refreshing chocolate shake. Then it was off to a movie with hot dogs, popcorn, soda, and candy.

What a fabulous adventure!

Finally she wobbled home with her husband and collapsed into bed. He leaned over and lovingly asked, "Well, dear, what was it like being ten again?"

One eye opened. "You idiot, I meant my dress size."[2]

True listening goes to a much deeper level than merely hearing. The words we use may mean one thing on their own, but the way we arrange those words and the tone and body language associated with those comments may have a much deeper message that we need to hear, understand, and respond to. Listening takes time, attention, and eye contact. It can't be done on the run. A couple needs daily, sit-down, face-to-face time to learn what is on each other's mind and to respond appropriately and effectively. If you really want to know your spouse and meet his or her needs, it can only be done by truly hearing the heart—his or her honest concerns and genuine desires. Close the laptop, put down the bills, stop cooking dinner, turn off the TV, and focus. Take time to learn how to listen to your spouse. What words does he or she use when in distress? What tone of voice is associated with each emotion? Does your spouse talk faster or slower, higher or lower, when happy or sad? What about body language—posture, gestures, arms, legs? What does calm look like? Or anxiousness? What does distracted and flighty look like? Listening is an art. Become a student of your spouse so you can communicate more clearly and fully hear what he or she is saying to you.

Be Creative

In demonstrating your love, be creative. Kidnap your spouse for a spontaneous day away. Plan a surprise lunch date. Complete a major project around the house while your spouse is out, and then have fun with an elaborate unveiling. There are a million ways to creatively express your love to your spouse. One year, we used the *Simply Romantic Nights (Vol 1) Kit: Igniting Passion in Your Marriage* by Family Life.[3] This kit is a series of index cards that lay out a romantic evening for you and your spouse. You can plan these together or take turns surprising the other with a creative and thoughtful romantic evening. It's a wonderful way to keep the spark in your marriage. The problem with many marriages is that they get stuck in the humdrum normal routine of life. Don't forget to stop and smell the roses. They smell so much sweeter when you're with the one you love.

For our fifteenth anniversary, we were able to get away to Monterey, California, home of Pebble Beach and possibly the most wonderful place in the world. We love vacationing there.

This was one of those incredible forty-eight-hour getaways. While we were there, we had breakfast served to us in bed. When it arrived, Jerolyn quickly grabbed the tray from the hotel personnel, which I (Jim) thought was odd. But stranger still, she proceeded into the bathroom. Now I am not much in the kitchen, but I do know not to combine the food and the bathroom, no matter how luxurious the bathroom is. Quickly, she replaced the napkin ring holder with a wonderful new wedding band for me. She had never really liked the one from our wedding and always felt it wasn't the classy look she wanted for me. What a surprise! Now understand, gift-giving is not Jerolyn's love language, and on top of it, she's very frugal. For her to lavish me with such a gift blew me away. She is amazing.

You don't have to plan trips or gifts, just keep your eyes open to fun moments with your spouse. When we were in our apartment in Columbus, Ohio, we had only been married about a year. Jerolyn was and is so practical that if a mess was made, it only meant that it would have to be cleaned up. So I (Jim) was shocked that she actually delivered on her promise of flinging her loaded spoon of mashed potatoes. They not only hit me, they stuck to the wall behind me. War was on and, in a smaller version of *Animal House*—FOOD FIGHT! Food was everywhere, but the laughter, fun, and memories were well worth the work of cleaning it all up. We have such a great time together. We simply love laughing with one another. There is nothing like sharing pure joy with the one you love.

Some creative acts of love can take more time to plan, while others require little planning at all but reap huge results. Taking a few moments out of your day to stop and think about how to show your love to your spouse in a unique way is a small price to pay for limitless benefits.

Pray

Pray for and with your spouse. While this may not seem like much, it is the greatest demonstration of love you can give to your spouse. E. M. Bounds said, "Prayer is our most formidable weapon, . . . [making] all else we do efficient."[4] Lifting your spouse to the Almighty is placing your most precious love in the hands of the one who created that love. Let your spouse know you are praying for her. Ask him how he wants you to pray each day and then be faithful in doing so. I (Jerolyn) know that Jim carries a lot of weight on his shoulders. He is the spiritual and administrative leader of a church. That is a tremendous responsibility to carry. On top of that, the church is in the middle of purchasing a building, so there are real estate brokers, architects, and government agencies to deal with. He has to wear many hats in his job—preacher, negotiator, counselor, community figure, evangelist, pastor, and writer in addition to being a husband and father. I can't do any of those jobs for him. But I can pray for him. By doing so I am reaching out to the Lord and asking him to supply my husband's every need. By faith, I know he will do it. There is no greater gift I can give my husband than to lift him up to the one who supplies the strength to face any and every situation.

Pray with your spouse, as well. One of the sweetest moments in our marriage happened when we were praying together. We were contemplating a church plant in a new area of Sacramento. Our friend, Jeff, who is an architect, brought over the land use plans for that area so we could pray over it and seek God's will. I (Jerolyn) remember putting the kids to bed while Jeff explained the symbols on the map to Jim. After Jeff left, we sat down at our dining room table and poured over the map, dreaming together about a life for us and for the new church in this area called Natomas. Then we decided to pray. We spread our hands across the map to cover the entire region and then bowed our heads. I waited for Jim to begin the prayer, but he was silent for a very long time. I finally opened one eye to take a peek at him. What I saw told me we were doing exactly what God wanted us to do by planting this church. Jim's shoulders were shaking as he began sobbing for the lost souls that had not even moved into this area yet. The fact that for many of them, their eternal address was going to be hell instead of heaven broke my husband's heart. Prayer was happening, and we hadn't even spoken a word. We shared a very special moment of crawling together on our knees to the very throne of God and praying for our future neighbors, grocers, store owners, doctors, and friends. And we prayed that our Lord would prepare us to meet the challenge of his work in Natomas. Whether you pray together or separately, it is imperative that you keep each other before the throne.

Pay

Pay the price, whatever the cost. Paul admonished in Ephesians, "Husbands, love your wives, just as Christ loved the church and gave himself up for her" (5:25). In any relationship, there is give and take. But with spouses, you must be willing to give everything you have and everything you are for your spouse if that is what it takes. I (Jim) can be a pain on this point about the covenant and am usually pretty hard on men in general because I do not believe we have done our part in keeping our end of the covenant much of the time. Men, we are the spiritual leaders (this was addressed in another section concerning our responsibility in that role), but we must take the leadership in honoring, loving, and cherishing our brides like our lives depend on it. Many times we have abdicated our responsibility and failed miserably because we don't understand or choose to ignore the high calling we have as husbands. I know this has been said more than once in this book, but Christ loved the church and was willing to literally die for her. Paul stated that this is exactly how we should live and love our wives! Jerolyn and I preach this hard to our own children. They know that both Dad and Mom really do buy into this and are willing to die for the covenant marriage that God has orchestrated and designed and that Christ has commanded be established.

Marriage is a sacrificial commitment. When you take this other person into your life, you no longer live for yourself, but you live to make his or her life fulfilled. Anne Lamott said, "A good marriage is where both people feel like they're getting the better end of the deal."[5] That happens through each spouse looking out for the other. Jim was in graduate school when we first married. To pay the bills, he worked at UPS as a morning sorter—loading the trucks to go out on deliveries. That meant that most days he was at UPS by 4:00 a.m., and at Christmastime, starting time could be 2:30 a.m. He'd come home, change, and go to school—sometimes not getting home until late into the evening. It wasn't ideal and certainly was an exhausting schedule, but Jim was willing to do whatever he had to in order to provide a roof over our heads and food to eat. I (Jerolyn) appreciated that he would make such sacrifices to take care of me. And he has continued to make those kind of sacrifices throughout our marriage.

But paying the price can fall in many areas of your marriage, not just in paying the bills. Loving another person means that you will do whatever it takes to make his or her life better; that you will lay down your own dreams, so your spouse's can be met; that you will protect your spouse from all harm; that you will be by his or her side through joy and sorrow—whatever the cost. Walter Wangerin, Jr. commented on 1 Corinthians 13, the love chapter, this way: "The apostle Paul didn't say that love bears some things, that love believes only in the best things, that love hopes for a reasonable period of time, or that it endures for a while. No, love is a divine absurdity. It is unreasonable. Paul said, 'Love bears *all* things, believes *all* things, hopes *all* things, endures *all* things.' Love is limit*less*."[6]

Whether it's little sacrifices or large, they all are acts of placing your spouse's needs and wants in front of your own. This can be a tough principle to follow if you are the only one in the relationship following it. It takes even more sacrifice. But when both spouses are on the same page in living to give their all to the other and his or her needs, a balanced, healthy relationship is created.

Serve

Serve rather than being served. Too often a spouse will want to live the "give and take" method of marriage and end up being only a taker. Choosing to serve your spouse is another way of reducing your selfishness and thinking of the other person first. We are taught in the Scriptures to serve one another. Who better should you be serving than your spouse? In fact, if you are out serving everyone but your spouse, you have a serious love issue. Too often, one spouse can get caught up in too much work in his or her job or too much time volunteering and neglect quality time with his or her spouse. Not only do both partners miss out on time with one another, but the neglected spouse can develop resentment against the other's job and commitments. While you must put in time at your job to do it well, and while volunteering for the church or other organizations is a worthy pursuit, neither of these should take away essential time with one another. It's tough to build a relationship with someone who only passes you going in or out of the door. Giving the best of yourself to serve others is a way of devaluing your spouse. Your husband or wife should be your number one service project of love.

Some couples have the time to serve each other, but they struggle with feeling that service is demeaning or degrading. Serving your loved one is quite the opposite. It is actually a beautiful act of humbling yourself to express the love of Christ to the person you love most in this world. Take time to do little acts throughout the day. Make not just your side of the bed, but your spouse's as well. Clear all the dinner dishes from the table. Occasionally do whatever chores your spouse normally does. Offer to get a snack or give a back rub when he or she looks tired, stressed, or worn out. This isn't rocket science, but it is intentionality. You have to take the time to look for ways to meet your spouse's needs or wants, and then do it. I (Jerolyn) absolutely love when Jim offers to cook dinner, do the dishes, or throw in a load of laundry for me. Jim appreciates when I do the deep-cleaning chores around the house, offer to get him something to drink when I'm getting up, or when I put fresh, clean sheets on the bed. You see, these aren't big, time-consuming activities, but simple acts of love. Don't get so caught up in serving the world and its needs that you neglect being a servant to the very special person beside you in bed.

Encourage

Another way to demonstrate your love is by being an encourager. We need to be each other's number one cheerleader. It is so easy to get caught up in criticizing your spouse. For some reason we think that everything he or she does reflects back on us. So we constantly want to improve our spouses by increasing their strengths and minimizing their weaknesses. By doing so, we become their coach and critic rather than the one applauding the loudest. We all desire to be told we are doing a good job. And when it comes from a spouse, the praise means even more. It's one thing to say you love someone. However, love can overlook many imperfections. But when you give praise to your spouse for something he or she did, it rings louder than praise from anyone else because you are the most important audience in his or her life, second only to God. And your praise says you not only love your spouse, but you are proud of him or her and what he or she does. For a man, this increases the respect factor. For a woman, it increases the feeling of being cherished and appreciated.

In his book *Empowered Leaders*, Hans Finzel, president of Worldventure, tells about his wife's role in helping him run the Vienna Marathon:

Donna would not let me give up. That was literally true! She and a friend took public transportation all over Vienna (with our son in a stroller), literally chasing me by following a map that I had drawn with estimates of when I would be at various places on the marathon run. At each checkpoint, she would be waiting for me with cheers and smiles and words of encouragement; then I would have a new burst of energy to keep going. Just as in that marathon, Donna in these middle years is right there with me, cheering me on and believing in me.[7]

What a way to finish the race of life—side-by-side, cheering each other on to the finish line.

Praise should not just be given *to* your spouse, but also said in public *about* your spouse. Michael Hyatt, chairman and former CEO of Thomas Nelson Publishing posted on his blog five reasons for speaking highly of your spouse in public:[8]

1. "You get more of what you affirm."

Most people like to be affirmed for the good things they do. When it's genuine and not manipulative, affirmation can be a powerful way to motivate others.

2. "Affirmation shifts your attitude toward your spouse."

Words can create or destroy, build up or tear down. We naturally want to align our actions and attitudes with our words. Start speaking well of your spouse, and your actions and attitudes will follow.

3. "Affirmation helps strengthen your spouse's best qualities."

Positive reinforcement is a powerful motivator. When others notice a positive change, it gives us the resolve to continue. Your affirmation will only enhance your spouse's character.

4. "Affirmation wards off the temptation of adultery."

Speaking positively about your spouse signals that you are in a happy marriage. Others are less likely to see you as "available" when you publicly praise your spouse.

5. "Affirmation provides a model to those you lead."

Those you lead will see your attitude toward your marriage as a demonstration of how you treat those you value the most. You earn trust by speaking well of your spouse.

Criticism easily rolls off of the tongue. Allow praise to dominate your conversations. Your spouse probably knows his or her weaknesses. Let your spouse know you see his or her wins.

Trust

Demonstrating trust creates an incredible intimacy in your relationship. You demonstrated trust when you first married one another. Genesis 2:24 says, "For this reason a man will leave his father and mother and be united to his wife, and they will become one flesh." The act of leaving your parents' home and joining together as one is the first act of trust in your marriage. You are demonstrating that you have faith in the other person to be loyal and committed to you and that he or she will return that loyalty and trust. Remember as a child playing the trust game? You stand stiff as a board and fall backward into someone's arms. That is the kind of trust you need to have in your marriage. You should know that no matter what happens, your spouse will be there to catch you every time, not just in the good times. But that kind of trust is built over time as you catch each other when one of you falls.

As the marriage continues, trust must be demonstrated again and again. I (Jerolyn) love when I ask Jim to do me a favor, such as picking up some milk. Even though he's had a busy day, he remembers to do it. It shows me that I am important to him and he loves me enough to remember to meet my needs. That is just a small act, but it builds my trust in him for the larger ones: trusting him to care for our family financially; trusting him with the physical care of our children; trusting him in making decisions that affect our future; trusting him to remain faithful to me and our marriage. Over the years, in small and big acts, Jim has shown me that I can trust him to love me, care for me, put my interests and needs first, and truly make me a priority in his life. It helps me feel extremely close to him. I know he has my back, and I trust him implicitly. And in return, I remain close to him and live a trustworthy life for him.

Date

Dating your spouse keeps the romance and newness alive. We recommend three kinds of dates — weekly, quarterly, and annually. The weekly dates are just to connect with one another face-to-face every seven days. Of course you should be connecting daily in some way, but this is a bit more special and for an extended amount of time. We (Jim and Jerolyn) are independent enough at this stage in our lives that we love to go out to dinner and a movie or to the theater. But when our children were little, it was expensive to get a babysitter. So we would put the kids to bed, eat Chinese takeout on our bed and watch a movie together or sit and talk. Even today, we love to sit outside on our back patio and talk around the world and back again. Sometimes we talk about the kids or the church. Other times we dream—about places we want to visit, things we want to do, or about what God has in store for us. Without some kind of weekly date, it's too easy to forget the reason you chose to marry this person.

Once a quarter we like to get away overnight. It's fun and adventurous. Go see different places, experience new things together. Financially this one may be a stretch, but it is worth saving up to do. And you can find some amazing deals to keep costs down. Even house sitting for friends gives you a new location to hang out. You are not focused on things you need to do in your own house, so you can focus on each other. Enjoy one another and remember why you chose to live the rest of your life with this person.

The annual date is all about the conversation. We like to go to a special, nice restaurant. We dress up and look extra nice for each other. Then over a beautiful meal, we have our state of the marriage discussion. We talk about how our marriage is doing, needs being met or not met, and how we can improve it.

However you choose to demonstrate your love for your spouse, the key is to intentionally choose and do it on a regular basis. You will work hard and plan diligently to do things in your career. You should show even more diligence in your marriage. It is for a lifetime. Learn to appreciate how your spouse shows love and celebrate the fact that he or she is taking time and energy to do so. Pearl S. Buck said, "A good marriage is one which allows for change and growth in the individuals and in the way they express their love."[9] Living out your values through demonstrating your love will grow your marriage in ways you never anticipated.

Next Steps

Questions

1. What are some ways I have done a good job demonstrating my love for you?

2. What are specific ways I can better demonstrate my love for you?

Activities

1. Have your spouse make a list of his or her needs in your marriage.

2. Spend an entire day listening to your spouse. (Let him or her know you are going to do this and that you're not being unresponsive.)

3. Plan some creative ways to express your love at least once each week for a month.

4. Pray for your spouse every day.

5. Say one encouraging thing to your spouse every day.

6. Plan a date a week, an overnight getaway once a quarter, and a state of the marriage dinner.

nine

Strategy 4: Delight

Delight stands for sex and intimacy. Plenty is said about sex in our society today. It has become an obsession while somehow also maintaining a commonplace position. TV shows seem to assume that a couple will sleep together by the second or third date. And adultery is barely acknowledged as a problem except when exposed in Christian circles. But sex in marriage is rarely addressed or its value emphasized.

Sexual intimacy is a vital component in living out the values of your marriage. This is an area that no other person belongs in except you and your spouse. Many people are involved in your career; your neighbors make up your community; your extended family and your children inhabit your home. But the bedroom is for you and your spouse alone. No one says what happens there, and frankly, it's no one else's business. This is a time for you and your spouse to connect in a way that you never connect with any other human being. Be purposeful about your intimacy. Marriages that fall apart have often done so because intimacy left the relationship. Don't let that happen to yours. Use this precious gift from the Father to protect your covenant marriage from distancing or distraction.

Sex in marriage can be very complex depending on what experiences and potential baggage you have brought into your marriage bed. We (Jim and Jerolyn) suggest that where there is a significant amount of baggage, you seek marriage counseling to sort through those issues. Don't try to work them out yourselves. You are too close to the issue and need professional help to sort through everything. The need for counseling is nothing to shy away from or be ashamed of. Seeking help means you value your relationship and want the very best for it. And that is something to celebrate.

Then there are the stages of life we must deal with. I (Jerolyn) was thinking about the adjustments we women have to make throughout our lives and how that affects our sex lives. At first, it's the adjustment of early marriage. You and your husband are learning how to live with each other and meet each other's needs. Then usually come the children. They are the ones who always want your attention and especially drain mommy of her time and energy. Someone once said, "A little sex makes little kids and little kids make little sex." Next, those children grow into teenagers who don't have normal schedules and force you to become creative with intimate times with your husband. Then comes menopause when you struggle with a decreasing libido. With all those changes throughout life, I figure there's about eighteen months between when the kids are gone and when menopause sets in that sex and intimacy is absolutely amazing! It's a challenge, but it's not insurmountable to experience all God desires for your marriage.

But if you have the complexities pared down, intimacy in marriage can be very fulfilling and fun. Some of us grew up in a very conservative environment where sex was not talked about at all or very little. And if it was, it was in hushed tones. Even as a boy, my (Jim) parents almost made it sound evil and bad. I know they were trying to protect me from sex before marriage, but it really wasn't talked about as a beautiful experience between husband and wife. It is often said jokingly, but in all honesty, that many young women have been told that sex is dirty, ugly, and gross—they need to save it for their husband (laugh inserted here). Many of us who grew up in the church had a don't-talk policy about sex. Instead the church has allowed the media and society to teach our children (not to mention the adults) about it. But the church must not remain silent. Sex is a biblically based activity that God has ordained. In Genesis 1 and Matthew 19, God and Jesus talk about sex. They say that a husband and wife become one flesh. That is sex. Sex is God-designed, and like everything else he created, he said it is good. God said to be fruitful and multiply. Your momma and daddy got together and said,

"Let's be fruitful," and look at all of us fruit. God is incredibly creative. We should all be screaming, "Yea, God! Thanks for sex!" In the boundaries of marriage, God was creative, and we agree that it is good.

The great thing about sex is that God designed it to be experienced between one man and one woman. This is also the tricky part about sex. In Genesis, it says that God made man from the dust of the earth, and he took a rib out of man and made woman. God made men and women in totally different ways, and he also gave us different needs and desires—in life and in the bedroom. What a man thinks his wife needs or desires from sex isn't necessarily what she wants because he is looking at the situation from his perspective. And the same is true about the woman's view of a man's desires. For example, a man is stimulated visually. He loves to look at his wife. He enjoys the curves, the peaks, and the valleys. He wants to see what you are giving him. That is one reason why it is so important to dress modestly in public, as we are told in 1 Timothy 2:9. Paul said, "I also want women to dress modestly, with decency and propriety." Wives, we have a responsibility to keep ourselves covered in public. But when we're with our husbands, we can let them see all they want. And they want it all.

Every wife has experienced turning her husband on in ways that seem strange—leaning over to remove something from the oven, bending across the table to clear the dishes, or walking in a dress and heels down a hall toward him. All these give him glimpses of parts of you that he wants to touch. I (Jerolyn) have always said, "It don't take much." And that is true. Your husband is stimulated with a glimpse, and he loves to look at your body. That is the way he is made, and you are completely free to let him look.

Sometimes a woman is uncomfortable letting her husband see her body. Bodies age and change. Unfortunately, society has made women feel bad about those changes. Thin, firm bodies in bikinis stare down at us from billboards, magazine covers, and endless commercials. And we have wrongly bought into the belief that the image they are portraying is the only one men desire. But they are wrong, and men, we need to be sure our wives knows that.

I (Jerolyn) happen to be built like a cereal box with appendages. When God handed out curves, I think he mistook me for a boy and completely passed me by. But that's OK, and you know why? Because I have a husband who loves my body just as it is with all its curveless "flaws." And he tells me all the time how beautiful my body is and how much he enjoys it. I never doubt that he loves to see me. Men, tell your wives how beautiful they are to you and what you love about them. They'll probably blush and say, "Stop it." But don't. They need to hear those words from you.

Scripture even demonstrates how you as the husband can help your wife feel more accepted. See Song of Songs 4:1–7:

How beautiful you are, my darling! Oh, how beautiful!
Your eyes behind your veil are doves. Your hair is like a

flock of goats descending from Mount Gilead. Your teeth are like a flock of sheep just shorn, coming up from the washing. Each has its twin; not one of them is alone. Your lips are like a scarlet ribbon; your mouth is lovely. Your temples behind your veil are like the halves of a pomegranate. Your neck is like the tower of David, built with elegance; on it hang a thousand shields, all of them shields of warriors. Your two breasts are like two fawns, like twin fawns of a gazelle that browse among the lilies. Until the day breaks and the shadows flee, I will go to the mountain of myrrh and to the hill of incense. All beautiful you are, my darling; there is no flaw in you.

The husband is telling his sweetheart that she is the only one for him and there is no other woman that can compare with her. Your wife needs to hear that. Tell her, and let your actions show that you mean it. Your wife knows if you are checking out other women. She knows if you really mean that she is the only one. In a sermon on marriage, I (Jim) told my congregation that I see my wife as both beautiful and godly. A woman in the congregation e-mailed to me the following: "Just a quick note to tell you how wonderful it was to hear you speak of your wife the way you did! I wish I had the words to express how much of a positive impact that makes for me to hear that kind of love, respect, and most importantly 'sexual' interest in one's spouse expressed by my pastor—it's a breath of fresh air."

Every wife wants to be wanted and desires so desperately to hear her husband say he desires her. Affirm your wife's place in your heart and your absolute devotion to her as being the only woman for you. She needs that assurance.

With the intensity that a man is turned on by visual stimulation, a woman is attracted to emotional advances and gentle touch. Women want to be romanced. We love to hear sweet nothings whispered in our ears. We love to be told we are beautiful. We melt when our husbands sweep our hair to the side and place light kisses on our necks. (Well, some women giggle and squirm because they are ticklish, but you get the idea.) We want to receive gifts—sometimes physical ones and sometimes in acts of service. I (Jerolyn) love when Jim does little things for me around the house. I feel his emotional connection to me through his actions. Of course, the occasional box of chocolates or bouquet of flowers never hurts. We simply want to be swept away by Prince Charming and treated like a princess.

Another aspect of the emotional stimulation a woman needs is to feel completely accepted by her husband. A woman cannot feel freedom in lovemaking if negative comments are lingering in her mind. When she hears comments like, "Is that all you did today?" "Why don't you lose weight?" "I can't believe how much money you spend!" or "That is so stupid!" any sense of romance is destroyed. Her knight in shining armor becomes either a tyrannical dictator or scolding parent. Every woman has room for improvement, and we all know our own shortcomings. But what we don't need is for our lover to point out those areas to us. We need our husbands to accept us in the midst of our progress, right where we are today. Then and only then can a woman freely give herself to her husband.

Women are not off the hook here either. Our husbands need to feel our acceptance, too. But too often wives can be extremely critical. Our husbands may have barely walked through the front door after a long day at work when we can start in. "Why don't you find a better paying job?" "You never spend enough time with the kids!" "This house is falling apart." You may still have sex after that because he needs the physical release, but believe me, there will be no emotional intimacy. You just emasculated him with your words. Before there can be intimacy in the bedroom, there must be love in your words. Be kind and gentle, not critical and harsh. Paul instructed the church at Colosse, "Therefore, as God's chosen people, holy and dearly loved, clothe yourselves with compassion, kindness, humility, gentleness and patience. Bear with each other and forgive whatever grievances you may have against one another. Forgive as the Lord forgave you. And over all these virtues put on love, which binds them all together in perfect unity" (Col. 3:12–14). When you soften your words, you will be amazed at the physical and emotional connection you can have with your husband.

Men and women are different people with different likes and dislikes, and our bodies and minds work in different ways. What works for one does not work for the other. Men, what works for your wife today may not work the same way next month. You may never understand why your spouse's preferences are the way they are. You don't need to. Simply learn to recognize the differences and appreciate each other for who you are.

The secret to great intimacy in sex is communication. Let your spouse know what things you like in the bedroom and what you don't like. Although sex is personally satisfying, the ultimate act of intimacy is to meet the other person's needs. To allow your spouse to express that kind of love to you, you must be willing to be open and honest about what you want to experience. Women, sit down with your husbands and talk to them about sexual intimacy. So much of the time men just don't think about intimacy from their wives' perspective. Please help them understand. Allow me (Jim) to be really direct here: We men do not know and please do not expect us to know. Please do not play that game with us—the one where we're just supposed to know, and if we don't, we must not love you.

Husbands and wives, have a heart-to-heart discussion that is not "in the moment," where you both share what you enjoy about sex and the parts you don't enjoy as much. Ask your spouse, "What do I do that is romantic?" Do you know what turns your spouse on? Ask your spouse and tell him or her to be specific.

And women, be careful to avoid negative communication. Let your husbands know you want to be with them. It can get pretty old if he asks for sex, and you roll your eyes and say with a heavy sigh, "OK." Or don't think you can hide it from your husband when you are mentally making out your grocery list or deciding what color to paint the ceiling. Be fully engaged in the moment. This is supposed to be the man with whom you have pledged to spend the rest of your life. Find pleasure in delighting him and in learning about what brings him pleasure.

God gave us sex not only for procreation, but also for our enjoyment. You can't read Song of Songs without recognizing that God wants you to enjoy intimacy with your spouse. By communicating desires, you are setting yourselves up for the best enjoyment possible. Columnist and comedian Dave Barry once said, "I believe it was Shakespeare, or possibly Howard Cosell, who first observed that marriage is very much like a birthday candle, in that 'the flames of passion burn brightest when the wick of intimacy is first ignited by the disposable butane lighter of physical attraction, but sooner or later the heat of familiarity causes the wax of boredom to drip all over the vanilla frosting of novelty and the shredded coconut of romance.' I could not have phrased it better myself."[1] So be creative to keep those flames burning.

Sometimes couples like to create a fantasy. For men it is often a scene—some location or something different you want your wife to be or do. For women it is often more of a romantic atmosphere and time period. Maybe she just wants to have a romantic getaway or vacation when you can both relax and have no one else around. Be considerate and don't force your spouse to do anything that makes him or her uncomfortable. The point is that you need to let your needs and desires be known. Be sure to take time on your marriage trip to be completely honest about your needs and your spouse's needs. You will be amazed at how your intimate times will be so much better when they're focused on satisfying your spouse's desires.

One of the greatest acts of intimacy is when husband and wife serve one another. And what better place to serve your spouse and meet his or her most personal needs than in the bedroom? But just as you discuss making a budget—having a plan—you need to do the same with sex. Spontaneity is nice but so often not realistic. The movies may make sex out to be one way, but this is reality TV. To truly meet each other's needs, you must come up with a plan.

Meeting each other's needs requires each of you to live self-lessly. Scripture clearly instructs us to surrender to one another as our body is not our own. Look what Paul had to say to the Corinthians on this subject:

> Now for the matters you wrote about: It is good for a man not to marry. But since there is so much immorality, each man should have his own wife, and each woman her own husband. The husband should fulfill his marital duty to his wife, and likewise the wife to her husband. The wife's body does not belong to her alone but also to her husband. In the same way, the husband's body does not belong to him alone but also to his wife. Do not deprive each other except by mutual consent and for a time, so that you may devote yourselves to prayer. Then come together again so

that Satan will not tempt you because of your lack of self-control. (1 Cor. 7:1–5)

In the area of sexual intimacy, we need to be less selfish and more giving. Too often, one spouse makes inappropriate demands; but many simply deny the other spouse and treat sex as if it is only about him or her and his or her needs, and do so with a selfish attitude. Learning to surrender to Scripture is learning to serve one another and being willing to sacrificially give to one another—again, in appropriate ways and actions.

Quit trying to get, and start giving. Serve each other. Men, you may think it is up to her. Nope. Men, as the leader, you need to lead in every area, including serving your wife. I (Jim) will say this again to make sure I am very clear about it. Men, when you begin to meet the needs of your wife, your needs are much more likely to be met.[2] When you treat her like a woman instead of a sex object, it is amazing what happens. Women, you need to serve him as well. Find out what he likes and serve him. None of us should do anything that is wrong or inappropriate, but we can and should enjoy and serve each other.

You may have never thought of Philippians 2:3 in this way, but focus on the words: "Do nothing out of selfish ambition or vain conceit, but in humility consider others better than yourselves." Daily we must choose to live as God designed us—in selfless love.

One man on his honeymoon got down on one knee, like when he proposed, and said, "I want to serve you like Jesus served the church." He pulled out a container of water and a towel and washed her feet as a symbol of his commitment to serve her for all of their marriage. Serving one another is the very heart of intimacy and must be carried into the bedroom.

Couples have sex an average of two to three times per week. I (Jim) think we as Christians should do everything better! But what happens when a man wants it every morning and the wife wants it every May? Stephen Arterburn and Fred Stoeker, in their book *Every Man's Battle*, say that for most men, a "heightened sexual desire takes only about seventy-two hours."[3] One couple mentioned that if they have average sex, the husband wants it again in twenty-four to forty-eight hours. But if they have great sex, he wants it again in about twenty-four to forty-eight hours. Ladies, it's how men are wired, and it's one of their basic needs that only you, his wife, can fulfill.

Life moves fast and furiously. Jobs are demanding. Children are demanding. Society is demanding as a whole. We just don't always have the time or the energy to keep up with a scheduled intimacy time. But there is something you can do. Come to an agreement on the minimum number of times you will try to have sex every week. Set a reasonable number. Three times a day is not reasonable. Once a day isn't reasonable either; and by the way, neither is once every other week. Come to a compromise you can both live with.

Once you have that number, commit to making it happen. Remember that this number is not set in stone. It may fluctuate due to life's obstacles, or it may increase because of some fun romance. Remain flexible but not lackadaisical. The idea is to remain purposeful about maintaining a healthy sexual relationship.

Even though this may seem a clinical approach to intimacy, it doesn't have to be. You can still set the romantic atmosphere or tease each other with little notes throughout the day. Just remember guys, when it comes time for the act, your hint from this morning is not enough. Bring your spouse with you on this journey. Your wife values conversation and face time. She wants to know in the moment that you are more interested in her as a person than as a sexual partner. So save some words for her when you get home from work. She needs you as her friend before you can be her lover.

And, ladies, don't make him always be the aggressor. You can seduce him as well. Those little hints throughout the day will mean so much to him. Even just a little secret message through sending a text or leaving a voicemail will make him feel special and anxious to get home to you that night. He will want to give to you his full attention, not just because he knows what is coming in the end, but because you have valued his desires throughout the day. Take turns being the one to make the first move. No one wants to always feel like he or she has to get the ball rolling. Take turns enticing each other.

Surprise each other by planning a romantic encounter. This lets your spouse know you made him or her a priority. Men, call your wife and tell her the babysitter is scheduled and the dinner reservations are made. She can take a shower or bath and relax for a bit while you run the kids to the sitter. Then after you get home from dinner, give her that something special you bought for her to wear. Next, break out the lotion and give her a gentle massage, then tell her what happens the rest of the evening . . . good things! Sometimes, however, it needs to just stop with the massage because she just wants to be held and loved. Remember, your wife does not run by a formula. Be sensitive.

Ladies, why don't you surprise your husband by meeting him at the door wearing only a coat? Visually, he would love it. One woman called her husband at work and when he asked her what she was doing she said, "I am sitting here thinking of you, and you can imagine what I am or am not wearing!" Believe me, he was in a hurry to get home to his bride.

Sex is a wonderful gift from our Creator and stands as an important component of a strong, healthy marriage. Be creative and make wonderful, intimate, passionate, and fun sex a priority in your marriage. God created it and desires it for you. The two became one flesh and God and the man and woman all said, "It is good!"

Next Steps

Questions

1. What do I do that delights you?

2. Is there anything I do in the bedroom that you would like me to stop doing?

3. Is there anything else you would like to add to our repertoire?

4. What is romantic to you?

Activities

1. Come to an agreement on how many times a week you will be intimate. (Remember, this is a soft number.)

2. Think of creative variety you can bring to the bedroom.

3. Read a book together on sex.

ten

Some Final Thoughts

We trust that this read has been more than just inspiring. So often we get inspired or excited but never really do anything with that inspiration. We trust that as we have attempted to once again write something practical, you have found it to be simply that: practical. Use the tools we have provided to write your own vision, values, and strategies to live out a godly covenant marriage.

We are blessed to help make a difference in the lives of couples and families. It is our desire that this resource will guide you on your journey, direct you to other resources, and encourage you to find what is necessary and best to live out the vision you have created for your marriage.

Please do not simply read and forget, but together take the time to develop these commitments. Your marriage is designed for more than getting through life together or raising kids, but for a life together of fun, enjoyment, laughter, commitment, hard work, and celebration of the big events and milestones and of the everyday life and love you share together. It is designed by God to be a great journey to experience so much of life together while investing and believing in one another. Working together on this is not only the most important priority you can have, but it's a lot of fun to share and dream together.

Other than loving God, this is the most important relationship of your life. It is the most important human relationship. Do not take it lightly. As we have stated, God himself created the mysterious and wonderful relationship of husband and wife. No other human relationship was created in this manner. He values the importance of the husband and wife relationship—spending their lives intertwined in the beautiful and holy covenant of marriage.

We pray that this book will be a tool to help couples reach the God-given potential each and every marriage is designed to be. We often say you must live a legacy long before you can leave a legacy. What better legacy can you leave your children, friends, and families than an amazing marriage for them to emulate? Go for it with all you have as you laugh, love, and live out God's vision and design for the two of you—a faith legacy for your marriage.

Devotions

The following devotionals are designed for you and your spouse to work through together on your marriage trip. Take time each morning to dig into God's Word and learn more about this wonderful adventure called marriage. Beginning each day in the Word will start off your discussions for that day on the right foot. You will be focused on what is honoring to God and fulfill his desire to place your spouse's needs before your own. (For more devotionals like these, go to Soul Thoughts at jerolynbogear.blogspot.com.)

Once you have completed the devotional, turn to the last page of each chapter in the book and reread the discussion questions. These questions will get you started on a productive dialogue for the day. Each chapter also includes activities for that chapter's topic. Plan ahead and bring those resources with you. Incorporate the questions and activities into your day. This marriage trip is a time to fully focus on each other and make your marriage as strong as it can be. Give yourselves completely to the process and enjoy the journey and each other.

The Covenant of Marriage

Submit to one another out of reverence for Christ. Wives, submit to your husbands as to the Lord. For the husband is the head of the wife as Christ is the head of the church, his body, of which he is the Savior. Now as the church submits to Christ, so also wives should submit to their husbands in everything. Husbands, love your wives, just as Christ loved the church and gave himself up for her to make her holy, cleansing her by the washing with water through the word, and to present her to himself as a radiant church, without stain or wrinkle or any other blemish, but holy and blameless. In this same way, husbands ought to love their wives as their own bodies. He who loves his wife loves himself. After all, no one ever hated his own body but he feeds and cares for it, just as Christ does the church—for we are members of his body. "For this reason a man will leave his father and mother and be united to his wife, and the two will become one flesh." This is a profound mystery—but I am talking about Christ and the church. However, each one of you also must love his wife as he loves himself, and the wife must respect her husband. (Eph. 5:21–33)

We are profoundly saddened by the number of affairs and breakups going on in Christian marriages around us. And it begins with one or both people consciously or unconsciously turning away from these commands God has placed on the marriage relationship—to submit and love.

Maintain that commitment. Period. No options, no plan B, no "if it works out." If you both have a conciliatory attitude, you can make it work.

So where does it all begin to fall apart? How do we avoid that first pull away? Success in marriage happens when there is surrender to Scripture. The Father has laid out very clearly the path to a healthy, thriving, and lasting marriage. Go back to the command in Ephesians 5:18: "Be filled with the Spirit." If we are living in our new selves and putting off the old, if we are living to please God, if we are living "not as unwise but as wise" (5:15), and if we are seeking God's will daily and are filled with the Spirit, then we can build a relationship of love and submission that is lasting and reflects the love that Christ has for his church. That is one strong bond no one can tear apart.

Further Thoughts

1. Read Genesis 2:18–24—the first marriage. What was unique about Adam and Eve's marriage that is symbolic of the marriage covenant?

2. What is the correlation between the success of your marriage and your daily walk with the Lord?

3. Read Hosea 1–3. Here is the story of a marriage that symbolizes the love Christ has for his bride, the church. What can you learn from Hosea for your marriage? List the attributes of Hosea. For a contemporary novel based on Hosea, read Francine Rivers' book, *Redeeming Love*.

4. Read 1 Corinthians 13 together and spend time thanking the Lord for the spouse you have the privilege of loving. Ask the Lord to help you love your spouse even better.

5. Is your marriage hanging on by a thread? Humble yourself before the Lord, confess and ask forgiveness for your part of the problem, pray for your spouse, and be sure to stay right with the Lord every day. You can't control your spouse's spiritual walk, but you can control yours. Remain humble before the Master and be filled with his Spirit. Love and submit to your spouse.

Father, we want to remain committed and strong in this marriage partnership we have chosen. Teach us how to do it well, and we again, before you, commit to remain faithful in our covenant to one another. Amen.

The Covenant of Marriage
Part 2

I tell you that anyone who divorces his wife, except for marital unfaithfulness, causes her to become an adulteress, and anyone who marries the divorced woman commits adultery" (Matt. 5:32).

Jesus took a stricter stance on the law than the actual law stated. He set the bar higher. Unfortunately, the statistics of those reaching that marriage bar, even among Christians and pastors, are low. We all must focus more on the covenant of marriage.

In the Old Testament, a covenant between two people was absolutely binding, and many of the rituals they went through are similar to rituals we use in wedding ceremonies today. The agreement was so binding between the two parties and to everyone around them that their very identities were exchanged so that they were forever inseparable from one another. That is how the marriage covenant is supposed to be—forever binding—a promise that is never broken in any way for any reason. And at the same time, one where God's grace and mercy are constantly on display.

The moral foundation of our society goes as its marriages go. God designed a format of one man and one woman forever for a very important reason—it's the only one that works. You won't always agree with your spouse on everything; you might not always like his habits. You won't wake up every single morning saying, "I am so excited to be married to this woman!" But you remain committed to him or her for your entire life. Nothing we've seen has convinced us that anyone has a better plan or that ignoring God's pattern produces better results. We chose to be in covenant with one another and that is where we'll remain.

Further Thoughts

1. For more on the Old Testament blood covenant, read Jim Garlow's book *The Covenant*.

2. Look up other Scriptures on divorce. Compare and contrast them with passages on marriage.

3. Is your marriage struggling? Look at your personal walk with God and your level of selfishness. You can't control your spouse's commitment, but you can control yours. If needed, ask your spouse to go to counseling with you. It's never too late.

4. If you are preparing to get married, pray and consider long and hard. A covenant is forever. Are you ready to make that binding commitment?

Lord God, heal our marriage. Turn our eyes away from other options and away from our selfish desires and direct them toward the person we have committed our lives to. Bind us together, Lord, with cords that cannot be broken.

The Life of Marriage

For this reason a man will leave his father and mother and be united to his wife, and the two will become one flesh. . . . Therefore, what God has joined together, let man not separate" (Matt. 19:5–6).

There are two words in these verses that we want to focus on—*united* (*joined* in NASB) and *flesh*. *Joined* in the Greek is *kollao*: to glue, to glue together, cement, fasten together, to join or fasten firmly together, to join one's self to, or to cleave to. *Sarx* is the Greek word for *flesh* of both man and beasts: the soft substance of the living body, which covers the bones and is permeated with blood.

A man and a woman are spiritually glued together. It's a cemented bond done through a covenant ceremony. Whenever you glue two things together, you do not do it with the intention of separating them later. Your purpose is to have them bonded permanently. If it were just a temporary bond, you'd use tape. But glue forms a seal between the two items that unites them into one.

So many analogies to marriage can be taken from the use of the word *flesh*. Our flesh is the most vulnerable part of our body.

Even though it usually can't be pulled apart, it can suffer from tears, punctures, and hard falls. Any of these can cause a rip in the flesh. In the same way, the flesh of the marriage can be injured by outside things poking and prodding at it. The question is: Are you protecting your flesh from the hazards that can harm it?

The flesh is what covers the skeleton. In a marriage, the skeleton is your family. The bond of your marriage protects the foundation of your family, covers it, and holds it together as one unit. The question is: Is your marriage protecting the framework of your family? The framework is what protects the vital organs—the very souls of your family.

Finally, flesh is permeated with blood. Blood is a source of life; it pumps throughout the entire body. If any part of the body is not receiving blood, it will die. Jesus is the source of your life. If any part of your marriage is not filled with the life he gives, that part will die. Here's where the analogy breaks down—with a body, you may be able to amputate the dead part and save the rest. With a marriage, if any part of it dies, eventually, that part will affect all of the flesh and kill the marriage.

Fortunately, marriage is different from a body in another important way. The healing power of Jesus Christ can restore the dead parts and make the body whole again. Marriages do not have to limp around in a slow death, dragging dead parts. Seek healing through the living blood of Jesus Christ.

Further Thoughts

1. Research some Old Testament marriages. What made them strong? What were their weaknesses?

2. Study the Old Testament covenant. What does it entail?

3. Research other passages on marriage. List the characteristics of a biblical marriage.

4. Who do you know who has a strong marriage? Ask that couple what makes their marriage strong. If their answers are based on biblical principles, how can you apply them to your marriage? (Never apply a principle to your marriage that is not biblically sound.)

Lord, make our marriage impervious to the outside influences that would attempt to pull us apart. Keep us bound together in your power. Protect our family that we may live a united front till the very end. Amen.

Submit and Love

S ubmit . . . love . . ." (Col. 3:18–19).

Why do people have a difficult time with the call to submit and love within marriage? Maybe it's a desire for control. Paul expanded on this thought in Ephesians 5:22–24. He stated that the husband is the head of the wife as Christ is the head of the church. The way we read that passage is that the husband has a much tougher job leading the wife like Christ leads the church than she has in submitting to his authority and leadership. What a responsibility. A woman's entire well-being and future is placed on her husband's shoulders. That's a heavy weight to carry. The antonym of *submit* is *fight*. A union that is fighting is a civil war. What marriage could survive under those conditions? We should be fighting *for* our marriages, not *against* them.

Now here's why submitting can be so easy. Read the husband's responsibility: "Love your wives" (Col. 3:19). Again, Paul expounded on that thought in much greater detail in Ephesians 5:25–33. The husband is required out of his love for his wife to lead her in the Word. Her holiness is partially his responsibility. He is to guide her to the holy life that God requires and protect her from sin. A husband is to love his wife like he loves his own body—feeding and caring for her. The entire duties of a husband to his wife reflect the relationship of Christ and the church. What a job to fulfill and burden to carry. If only all men and women could realize that by taking on the responsibility God gave them, they would strengthen their marriages and their families would be a place where God's grace and salvation can be experienced.

Further Thoughts

1. The first line of defense in your marriage is your own commitment to the Lord. Are you walking with God in full devotion? He wants complete surrender in all areas of your life, not just the convenient ones. Let him have everything.

2. Second, are you being the spouse God called you to be? What needs to change? How are you going to start making that happen? Do you need tools or accountability? Get them!

3. If we had to boil down marriage into one word it would be *selflessness*. If you give all of yourself to a person who loves you, you will receive back all you need. Placing each other second only to God is his only plan.

Lord, a horrible plague is attacking our marriage. Show us how to live out the sacred covenant you have designed and to keep it holy. Lord, we desperately need your help and guidance.

Take a Stand

Tear down your father's altar to Baal and cut down the Asherah pole beside it. Then build a proper kind of altar to the LORD your God on the top of this height" (Judg. 6:25–26).

Gideon's family had taken to worshiping foreign gods, and God wanted Gideon to do something about it. He was to tear down their altars and build new ones to the one true God. Gideon did it, but he was so afraid of what his family would think that he tore them down at night. He still had some growing to do in his trust of God, but he was experiencing a very real, human fear of rejection for his beliefs and for following God's ways.

We're experiencing similar challenges today. We're not literally tearing down Asherah poles, but other altars have been built into our lives that we must tear down and replace with the altar of the one true God. Maybe we have allowed the god of complacency to enter our lives. Or the deceiver. Or laziness or anger. Maybe it's a person who is taking all our time and thoughts. Maybe an activity or hobby. Sometimes very innocuous activities that in and of themselves are fine can begin to take a top drawer position in our priorities. There are all kinds of gods we allow to take over our lives, and maybe we don't even realize it is happening.

But when we allow those things to creep in, we are slowly pushing God aside.

Our God is a jealous God. He does not take being replaced lightly. The first commandment God gave to Moses was: "You shall have no other gods before me" (Ex. 20:3). Too often we hear that and think, "Well, I don't worship other gods. I worship the true God. I go to church; I pray." But whenever we place anyone or anything above God in our hearts, we worship that person or thing. God must take top priority in our lives—in all our thoughts, actions, motives, emotions, and decisions. He wants to be in every part of our being. And if he isn't, he will encourage us to tear down the altars and build the right one.

He may demand our respect and attention, but it is for our own good. If he is not Lord of our lives, if anything else steps in the place where he belongs, we choose a path that is outside of his will. It may be unpopular, but we must take a stand. He will be Lord with or without us. We must choose to stand with him.

Further Thoughts

1. Do you stand for God and his truth, or are you letting other things take priority?

2. What causes you to veer away from standing firmly with God?

3. How can you keep God first in your life?

4. What price do you need to pay to stand with God? Are you willing?

Father, I believe it is going to get harder and harder to stand with you. The world's philosophy is like a giant magnet enticing me to attach and conform. But my heart remains with you. Keep me close, Father. Even though it may be difficult, help me to stand in your truth and as your servant. Amen.

Hot, Warm, or Cold

O ur dear friend Luke, the doctor, and Demas send greetings. Give my greetings to the brothers at Laodicea, and to Nympha and the church in her house" (Col. 4:14–15).

The body of Christ has and always will fill the pews with a variety of believers at different stages of their walk with Christ.

Some will catch the fire quickly or gradually, but either way, their devotion is true and unwavering. They never turn to the left or right. Their hearts are pointed in one direction—the way of the Lord. The world appears black and white to them because they have decided for good rather than evil. Luke and Nympha were such people. Luke, the writer of the third gospel, gave his life for furthering the gospel of Christ. Luke often traveled with Paul on his missionary journeys, and it is believed that Luke died a martyr's death. He was a Gentile doctor, educated by the Greeks, who recognized the Messiah and surrendered to be his follower. Nympha, although not as well-known as Luke, gave just as much to the mission of Christ. She gave up the privacy and safety of her home and family to have a home-church meet there. She understood that with devotion comes sacrifice. Even though meeting in her home could have brought persecution, she was willing to give to her Lord all she had.

Others will take the name of Jesus, but their commitment rises and falls with the wind. They may or may not participate with the body because their Christianity is based on duty rather than heart. Full devotion is not in their vocabulary because they have never completely surrendered their hearts, minds, bodies, and souls to the Lord Jesus Christ. Self still wants to creep in to daily life, and the Christian label becomes simply a "get out of hell free" card in their practical lives. The Laodicean church is known as the lukewarm church in Revelation 3. God says that he'd rather we be hot or cold; but a lukewarm people he will spit out of his mouth (3:16). The people of the Laodicean church couldn't decide if they wanted their lives guided by God or by their wealth. They fell into the horrible trap that money can buy happiness and that's all that is needed for a meaningful life. But what they missed is that God works on completely different rules than the world. Money may buy temporary happiness, but serving the Master brings overwhelming joy and the hope of eternity with him.

Lastly, we have the cold—those who have seen the truth and have chosen to turn away from it. They may leave for several different reasons. In most cases, self takes over. The Christian walk asks for too much sacrifice. Or maybe they were hurt by one believer and have lumped all of Christianity into one category and no longer want anything to do with it. Or maybe they feel they have done so much wrong that they could never be forgiven or accepted by this group of believers, so they never try. Or maybe they feel judged by believers. There are so many avenues to turn away from a life with Christ. All of them lead to the same place—eternity without the Father.

Even though Paul sent greetings from Demas, we know that Demas later deserted Paul. In 2 Timothy 4:10, Paul said that Demas left him "because he loved this world." The draw of the world is strong. The Enemy has made it very enticing. It takes diligence to stay in close relationship with Christ and the body of believers while avoiding the temptations and pleasures of the world. If we don't, we will destroy our faith and walk away from the Lord.

You must remain strong and determined in your relationship with and service to the Lord Jesus Christ. You have one life to live. Choose to be fully devoted to the Master.

Further Thoughts

1. Which are you—hot, warm, or cold?

2. Look at various people in the Old and New Testaments. Were they hot, warm, or cold? Explain.

3. Who do you want to be?

4. What does it take to live a life on fire for Christ?

Lord, I am a slave to you. Protect me from the temptations of the world. Holy Spirit, guide me in wise choices that will honor you and not my desires. Amen.

Marriage Attributes

Purity and reverence . . . gentle and quiet spirit . . . considerate . . . with respect . . ." (1 Pet. 3:2, 4, 7).

It's almost as if Peter was giving a formula for a great marriage. Look more closely at these attributes.

Purity and Reverence: Peter said we should live out our Christian life with holiness and a reverence for the awesomeness of God. Our God-view affects everything in our lives—the way we worship, the way we do our jobs, how we parent, and how we have relationships. Therefore, this is where we begin in having a great marriages—with our relationships with God.

Gentle and Quiet Spirit: We (Jim and Jerolyn) both are constantly working on this one. It does not come naturally to us. We have always admired older men and women who are so gentle and quiet that every time they speak, we stop and listen because we know words of wisdom are going to come. Maybe if we keep surrendering our mouths and opinions to the Lord long enough, by the time we're older, we'll be that gentle. In the meantime, we continue surrendering away. But our marriage won't wait until then, so we must keep a reign on our tongues and tempers. We must, by God's power and Spirit, maintain gentle spirits.

Considerate: If you take the time to meet each other's needs, your needs will be met. You don't have to always go after your own needs. Being considerate to another person will often bring about a reciprocal relation. Selflessness goes a long way to helping both people in a marriage feel fulfilled.

With Respect: Respect is huge in a marriage and one of the hardest attributes to maintain. Here is a person you know the best of anyone in the world, and your love and desire for him or her to succeed is great. You want your spouse to always come out on top in whatever he or she tries. So you tend to see not only all their strengths, but their weaknesses as well. And since you are so familiar with one another, you automatically believe you have the right to point out those weaknesses. Hopefully, your motivation is because you want your spouse to excel. Sometimes, it's because you are ashamed of or feel superior to him or her. The caution is, you are not perfect, and your spouse knows your weaknesses too. In a marriage, the same grace that Christ afforded to you so freely should be given to those you love and are closest to. Grace is probably the greatest form of respect you can ever give.

Further Thoughts

1. Look up the definition of each of the key words in this passage. Then find more Scriptures on each.

2. How did Queen Esther exemplify these attributes?

3. Which attribute do you already show? Which attribute do you need to work on this week?

4. Read about ways you are to guard your tongue. How does this apply to a great marriage?

Wife's Prayer: *Lord, first, help my relationship with you to be holy and reverent. Then through your Spirit's filling of a gentle and quiet spirit, help me to be considerate and respectful of my husband. Once again, I commit my marriage to you.*

Husband's Prayer: *Lord, first, help my relationship with you to be holy and reverent. Then through your Spirit's filling of a gentle and surrendered spirit, help me to be considerate and loving toward my wife. Once again, I commit my marriage to you.*

Quarterly Checkup

In business, models are written to maintain a successful corporation. Business plans are written, poured over, rewritten, and reviewed. If the company is veering away at all from the final goal and vision, corrections are made to plans and processes. Sometimes, completely new ideas must be implemented to stay in touch with a changing culture and the consumer's needs.

In many ways you need to treat your marriage much like a business in regard to reaching your goals. That includes having regular checkups to be sure you and your spouse are still on the same path with the same goals in mind. Earlier in this book, an annual state of the marriage discussion was introduced. This can tend to be a more celebratory discussion. The quarterly review is to help you focus on specific areas because an annual review may not be enough. The following questions are designed to create a discussion that will clarify if you are moving forward in your journey. These are questions to assist you. Do not feel like you have to answer all of them each time.

Find a quiet restaurant or put the kids to bed early, and spend time discussing these points at least four times a year. Don't put it off. Two people walking two different paths for too long will have a harder time getting back on track. Get on the same page now.

Ask each other these questions:

1. How are we doing as a couple in general?

2. How are you doing in your spiritual walk? What is God teaching you lately?

3. (For the husband) How can I be a better spiritual leader to you?

4. (For the wife) What areas in my role as wife am I doing the best in right now (respecter, submitter, tone setter)? How can I do better in the other areas?

5. How do I best show you that I love you?

6. (For the wife) On a scale of one to five, how am I doing showing that I honor you? How can I do this better?

7. (For the husband) On a scale of one to five, how am I doing to show you that I cherish you? How can I do this better?

8. On a scale of one to five, how am I doing to communicate with you in all areas of my life? What areas could I be more open to you in?

9. What are some ways that I have improved in demonstrating my love to you? What are some ways that I could do better?

10. How can I meet your needs better in the bedroom?

11. How am I doing in meeting your needs currently?

12. How have your needs changed?

13. What is your greatest need that I should be meeting? How am I doing? On a scale of one to five, how I am doing to meet your needs?

14. What would make me the best husband or wife for you?

15. Do you feel that I listen to you?

16. How am I becoming the spouse you need so that we can have the best marriage possible?

17. Is there any area in our marriage that you think we should especially focus on over the next three months?

Resources

Arterburn, Stephen and Fred Stoeker with Mike Yorkey. *Every Man's Battle: Winning the War on Sexual Temptation One Victory at a Time*. Colorado Springs: WaterBrook Press 2000.

Eggerichs, Emerson. *Love and Respect: The Love She Most Desires; The Respect He Desperately Needs*. Nashville: Thomas Nelson, 2004.

Family Life. *Simply Romantic Nights (Vol 1) Kit: Igniting Passion in Your Marriage*. Little Rock, Ark.: Family Life, 2006.

Feldham, Shaunti and Jeff. *For Men Only: A Straightforward Guide to Inner Lives of Women*. Colorado Springs: Multnomah, 2006.

Feldham, Shaunti. *For Women Only: What You Need to Know about the Inner Lives of Men*. Colorado Springs: Multnomah, 2004.

Garlow, James L. *The Covenant: A Bible Study*. Kansas City, Mo.: Beacon Hill 1999.

Gillham, Bill and Anabel. *He Said, She Said: Candid Conversations about the Making of a Great Marriage*. Eugene, Ore.: Harvest House, 1995.

Heald, Cynthia. *Loving Your Husband*. Colorado Springs: Navpress, 1989.

Heald, Jack and Cynthia. *Loving Your Wife: How to Strengthen Your Marriage in an Imperfect World*. Colorado Springs: Navpress, 1989.

Leman, Kevin. *Sheet Music: Uncovering the Secrets of Sexual Intimacy in Marriage*. Carol Stream, Ill: Tyndale, 2003.

Rosenau, Douglas. *A Celebration of Sex: A Guide to Enjoying God's Gift of Sexual Intimacy*. Nashville: Thomas Nelson, 2004.

Swindoll, Charles R. *Strike the Original Match*. Portland, Ore.: Multnomah, 1980.

Notes

Chapter One

1. "Marriage," Merriam-Webster, accessed November 30, 2011, http://www.merriam-webster.com/dictionary/marriage.

2. James L. Garlow, *The Covenant: A Bible Study* (Kansas City, Mo.: Beacon Hill, 1999), 16–22.

3. "Bill Cosby," Search Quotes, accessed November 30, 2011, http://www.searchquotes.com/quotation/That_married_couples_can_live_together_day_after_day_is_a_miracle_that_the_Vatican_has_overlooked/ 34371/.

4. *Indiana Jones and the Last Crusade*, Paramount Pictures (1989).

5. "Marriage," Quote Garden, accessed November 30, 2011, http://www.quote garden.com/marriage.html.

Chapter Two

1. "Marriage," Good Reads, accessed November 30, 2011, http://www.good reads.com/quotes/show_tag?name=marriage.

2. John F. MacArthur, Jr., *Different by Design: Discovering God's Will for Today's Man and Woman* (Wheaton, Ill.: Victor, 1997), 122.

3. Ibid.

4. Elizabeth Bernstein, "Meet the Marriage Killer," *The Wall Street Journal*, January 25, 2012.

5. Sydney Harris, "Thoughts at Large," *Pittsburgh-Post Gazette*, August 10, 1978.

6. "Hupotasso," Bible Study Tools, accessed November 30, 2011, http://www.biblestudytools.com/lexicons/greek/kjv/hupotasso.html.

7. Charles R. Swindoll, *Strike the Original Match* (Portland, Ore.: Multnomah, 1980), 20.

8. Susan T. Foh, *Women and the Word of God: A Response to Biblical Feminism* (Phillipsburg, N.J.: Presbyterian and Reformed, 1979), 200.

9. "Catherine Aird," Good Reads, accessed November 30, 2011, http://www.goodreads.com/quotes/show/1963.

Chapter Three

1. Gary Smalley, *Connecting with Your Husband* (Colorado Springs: Smalley, 2003), 18–19.

2. Shaunti Feldham, *For Women Only* (Colorado Springs: Multnomah, 2004), 23.

3. Emerson Eggerichs, *Love & Respect: The Love She Most Desires; The Respect He Desperately Needs* (Nashville: Thomas Nelson, 2004), 49–50.

4. Charles R. Swindoll, *Strike the Original Match* (Portland, Ore.: Multnomah, 1980), 51.

Chapter Four

1. Dietrich Bonhoeffer, *Letters and Papers from Prison* (London: SCM Press, 1953), 42–43.

2. "Jay Trachman," ThinkExist, accessed December 1, 2011, http://think exist.com/quotation/never_criticize_your_spouse-s_faults-if_it_weren/ 176868.html.

3. "Marriage Quotes," Smart Marriages, accessed February 24, 2012, http://www.smartmarriages.com/marriage.quotes.html.

4. "Marriage," Good Reads, accessed December 1, 2011, http://www.good reads.com/quotes/show_tag?name=marriage&page=2.

Chapter Six

1. Larry Crabb, *The Marriage Builder* (Grand Rapids, Mich.: Zondervan, 1992), 36–37.

2. Ibid., 93.

3. Peggy Noonan, "Welcome Back, Duke," *The Wall Street Journal*, October 12, 2001, http://online.wsj.com/article/SB122451174798650085.html.

Chapter Eight

1. Gary Chapman, *The Five Love Languages: The Secret to Love That Lasts* (Chicago: Northfield, 2010).

2. "What would you most like for your birthday?", Tension Not, accessed December 1, 2011, http://www.tensionnot.com/jokes/wedding_jokes/what_ would_you_most_your_birthday.

3. *Simply Romantic Nights (Vol 1) Kit: Igniting Passion in Your Marriage*, FamilyLife (2006).

4. E. M. Bounds, *Purpose in Prayer* (Radford, Va.: Wilder Publications, 2008), 27.

5. "Marriage," Good Reads, accessed December 1, 2011, http://www.good reads.com/quotes/show_tag?name=marriage&page=3.

6. Walter Wangerin, Jr., *As For Me and My House: Crafting Your Marriage to Last* (Nashville: Thomas Nelson, 1987), 81.

7. Hans Finzel, *Empowered Leaders* (Nashville: Thomas Nelson, 2002), 172.

8. Michael Hyatt, "Why Speaking Well of Your Spouse is So Important, accessed December 1, 2011, http://michaelhyatt.com/why-speaking-well-of-your-spouse-is-so-important.html.

9. "Marriage," Good Reads, accessed December 1, 2011, http://www.good reads.com/quotes/show_tag?name=marriage.

Chapter Nine

1. "Marriage," Good Reads, accessed December 1, 2011, http://www.good reads.com/quotes/show_tag?name=marriage.

2. Jack and Cynthia Heald, *Loving Your Wife* (Colorado Springs: Navpress, 1989), 16.

3. Stephen Arterburn and Fred Stoeker with Mike Yorkey, *Every Man's Battle* (Colorado Springs: Waterbrook, 2000), 64.

An Excerpt From

Faith Legacy
Six Values to Shape Your Child's Journey

by Jim and Jerolyn Bogear
Available Now!

THE LEGACY
OF CHARACTER

Historically, a legacy was something of value that was handed down from one period of time to another, from one generation of a culture to the next, or perhaps some object or heritage passed down through families. In raising our children, it's our desire to leave a much more significant legacy than material possessions or family traditions, even though those are certainly nice things to pass along. Our greatest desire is to pass along the legacy of *character*; specifically, the character of Christ.

Our modern culture seems to put very little emphasis on character. For example, we can look at the people elected into political office. They're not usually selected because of their character; they win because they promise the things we want to hear. And whom do our young people often idolize? Musicians, actors, and sports celebrities . . . and our young people rarely consider the character of these celebrities they adore; instead, they're applauding and envying their accomplishments and cultural status, not who they really are. Oftentimes celebrity character flaws, even though made public, are simply overlooked as being "their private life." While our children may still admire a celebrity's accomplishments, we can teach them to be discerning and look elsewhere to learn how to live a life of character.

As Horace Greeley, a New York newspaper editor in the 1800s, wisely observed: "Fame is a vapor, popularity an accident, riches take wing, and only character endures." Our character is the essence of who we are. As such, there is no greater legacy we can leave than that of character.

THE BEST MODEL OF CHARACTER

When it comes to character, there's no greater example than Jesus Christ. To believers, Scripture says "clothe yourselves with the Lord Jesus Christ" (Rom. 13:14). That means taking on His character. We, as parents, want our children to revere people who virtuously live what they say and say what they live. God-made-in-flesh showed us how to live virtuously while struggling in this earthly body. He faced the same trials and temptations we face in being a person of character. Oh, they sometimes come in different forms than they did in Jesus' day—TV, movies, the Internet—but they're still ways to pull us down to a level below "the best" God desires for us. If the Enemy can get hold of us in the area of our character, he has all of us.

Oliver Wendell Holmes said, "What lies behind us and what lies before us are tiny matters compared to what lies within us."

The greatest battle we face is the one within. Yes, the pressures outside our bodies are the temptations, but we must fight the carnal nature within, the element that strives to compromise our character standards. In God's Word, we find very specific guidance in how to deal with this struggle: "Be imitators of God, therefore, as dearly loved children and live a life of love, just as Christ loved us and gave himself up for us as a fragrant offering and sacrifice to God" (Eph. 5:1–2).

Leadership is a potent combination of strategy and character.
But if you must be without one, be without the strategy.

—*General Norman Schwarzkopf*

If we read further in the same passage, we can break down several issues and discover important questions to ask ourselves about how we're developing our own character:

But among you there must not be even a hint of sexual immorality, or of any kind of impurity, or of greed, because these are improper for God's holy people. Nor should there be obscenity, foolish talk or coarse joking, which are out of place, but rather thanksgiving. For of this you can be sure: No immoral, impure or greedy person—such a man is an idolater—has any inheritance in the kingdom of Christ and of God. (Eph. 5:3–5)

From this passage, we can draw several penetrating questions and observations:

- What are we filling our minds with from TV, movies, or the Internet?
- Are we focusing on pursuing "things" rather than pursuing God?
- Are we set apart from the world, rather than being of the world?
- How are we talking to others? Are we lifting people up or putting them down?
- Are we practicing gratitude or complaint?

It can't be any clearer: We can't have our feet both in heaven and in the world—it's either/or. As followers of Christ, we are called to be set apart in our character. God calls us to a higher standard, and if we choose to follow the way of the world and its desires and lusts, we will not receive our inheritance of heaven. That's heavy stuff and it thoroughly underscores the urgency and necessity for a Christlike character.

You can observe a lot just by watching.

—*Yogi Berra*

The Word continues: "Let no one deceive you with empty words" (Eph. 5:6). Those include the lies that the media and society are espousing and that we so easily give in to, promising we'll be happier, prettier, more popular, or more powerful. The Bible says "because of such things God's wrath comes on those who are disobedient" (v. 6). His wrath? Do we want to experience the anger of the almighty Creator of the universe? We can't even begin to imagine what that would be like. Kids think an angry parent is bad. This is the granddaddy of all angry parents and then some! It's eternal.

LEGACY TRIP IDEA #3

Our son Shay loves to golf, so we headed to the *Mecca* of golf on the West Coast, Pebble Beach. We had some great conversations about life and our core values, while attempting to conquer some challenging golf holes.

The passage closes with a very simple sentence that gives the solution to the whole issue: "Therefore do not be partners with them" (Eph. 5:7). Simple and effective: Don't partner with that stuff. Sin may be fun for a time, but the consequences are forever. We must ask ourselves and our children—is it really worth it? We know life can be tough, and the difficulties are not always of our own doing. Pain is imposed on innocent people every day. Despite this, we can choose to not live in filth or be pulled down into its dregs. *We* make the decision. We choose to succumb to the temptations around us for temporary satisfaction, or we choose to fight the battle within for an eternal reward. It begins with us, our own choices, and then we must do everything we can to help our children be successful in their battles too.

READY FOR BATTLE

Are we on our own in this battle? Absolutely not! We don't have to fight these battles alone.

Character is self-control mastered by truth. Galatians 5:23 tells us self-control is one of the nine fruits of the Spirit. It's not born of self-determination, bestowed upon us by parents or friends, or acquired by power or money. It's from the Holy Spirit, as He lives within us. Yes, we must choose to resist temptation, but the power to do so comes from living in the power of the Spirit of God. Stand in the truth, and the Truth will stand in you. If our focus is to live for Christ, who is absolute truth, then we'll receive our power from Him. Standing in the truth is a simple concept to grasp, but not as simple to live. Character is developed as a daily discipline. It's a victory, not a gift. There's a reason Jesus said, "If anyone would come after me, he must deny himself and take up his cross daily and follow me" (Luke 9:23).

How do we deny ourselves? First, set aside time to spend with our Lord. How many of us tackle 101 things to do in a day and then say, "I don't have time to spend with God." It's a matter of choice. He so desires to help us through the struggles of life, but we need to know who He is by learning about Him in His Word, so that we can know the way He would handle the situations we face. In studying His character, we can better mirror it and be shaped by it. But if we spend little or no time learning about Him and His character, we'll have no idea what it looks like. And if we focus only on the stuff of this world (which, by the way, is presently and temporarily under the control of the Enemy), then that is what will come to the forefront of our character.

Children, obey your parents in the Lord, for this is right. "Honor your father and mother"—which is the first commandment with a promise— "that it may go well with you and that you may enjoy long life on the earth." Fathers, do not exasperate your children; instead, bring them up in the training and instruction of the Lord.

—Ephesians 6:1–4

A great illustration of this principle comes from the Royal Canadian Mounted Police. One of their jobs is to locate counterfeit money. In all their training, they never look at one piece of counterfeit money—they look only at the real thing. They learn it inside and out, frontward and backward. That way, when they do see currency that doesn't line up with the real thing, they know it's false. This is the way we want to live! We don't need the world to teach us how to live. We don't even need the world to teach us how not to live. All we need is the Truth to show us how to live the truth. We want the Creator to teach us how to be the creation He meant for us to be.

Psalm 1 says, "Blessed is the man who does not walk in the counsel of the wicked or stand in the way of sinners or sit in the seat of mockers. But his delight is in the law of the LORD, and on his law he meditates day and night" (vv. 1–2). This daily discipline of being in the Word and allowing the Lord to work in our lives is not just to obtain head knowledge; heart change must happen too. The apostle Paul says to "be transformed by the renewing of your mind" (Rom. 12:2).

Second, practice "staying near the water." The one who's being transformed into the likeness of Christ by learning from Him and walking in His knowledge will be living like Psalm 1:3 describes: "He is like a tree planted by streams of water, which yields its fruit in season and whose leaf does not wither." Ever been driving along and seen fields and fields and more fields and then suddenly a group of trees? If they're growing naturally, they're probably standing alongside water. Nature knows where the source of life is—near water—where a tree gets its staying power. It can't live without water. Jesus Christ is our river of life. He's the one source who will empower us to thrive and be fruitful. When we stay close to Him, we're better able to fight the battles, make the right choices, and build our character.

Third, we must "share the wealth." Knowledge and personal transformation cannot remain in isolation. This is part of taking up our cross daily and following Him (Luke 9:23). We must take the Word of truth implanted within us during our time spent with the Lord and go share it with a dark world just like Jesus did. Does this mean we're calling for door-to-door evangelists? No, we're calling for people to live out the truth of Jesus Christ by walking as a person of character; a person who lives a life devoted to, committed to, and glorifying the Lord. We call them "Truth Walkers." It can be done in any career. We have to make money to live, but we live to minister. Part of the daily discipline is not seeing life as drudgery, but as an opportunity to glorify God in all we say, do, and think. The seeds we sow by living a life that glorifies God will direct others to the Kingdom.

CHARACTER IS THE FOUNDATION

Living a daily discipline of growing our character to be like Christ will prepare us for whatever comes our way. Some people think their character will step up a notch when they really need it; they think they don't need to worry about good character until crunch time. (And even though some may not espouse this philosophy, it certainly comes out in the way they live.) However, true character is revealed, not developed, in times of crisis.

Stephen is a great example of this principle. He was a man who lived for Christ. He fought for Him against the religious leaders who were persecuting the early church. In the end, he was stoned to death. When he was being stoned, Stephen could have renounced everything he had said and probably would have been allowed to live. But his character ran much deeper; when he was facing a crisis—even death—Stephen's character prevailed. The book of Acts recounts Stephen's last moments on this earth: "While they were stoning him, Stephen prayed, 'Lord Jesus, receive my spirit.' Then he fell on his knees and cried out, 'Lord, do not hold this sin against them.' When he had said this, he fell asleep" (Acts 7:59–60). Stephen's character remained firm in crisis because it was built on truth, not on his circumstance, and was matured over time.

A few years ago, Jerolyn's grandmother had a stroke and was in a coma for three days. When she awoke, her

LEGACY TRIP IDEA #4

Our oldest child, Lauren, loves drama and the theater, so we flew to New York City. What a great location for many lessons, as well as some incredible sights and wonderful plays.

memory was completely gone except for her husband's name and Jesus' name. She remembered nothing, including that she had three daughters and seven grandchildren. After her daughters spent several days reprogramming her mind every waking moment, she finally started to regain her memories. The very first memory to come back was Scripture. Isn't that awesome? The Word of God was so imprinted on her heart that it was the first thought to resurface. True character revealed in crisis.

JESUS, THE LEGACY OF LIFE

In raising our children, it's our desire to model Christlike character. But this can't be accomplished through sheer willpower. It must be through surrender to the transforming power of Jesus Christ and a passionate pursuit of Him. We daily walk in the discipline of becoming more like Him through surrender to His will and spending time in His Word. We give control to the truth, and He prepares our character to face whatever challenges we may encounter.

Are we saying that only believers in Jesus Christ have good character? Absolutely not. There are thousands of people who demonstrate good character every day—they are "good" people. But our true character will eventually be revealed because it's housed in the depths of our soul, where it's guarded by God or by the Enemy.

For example, take two bottles of water, one containing pure water and the other holding tainted water, and place several nuts and bolts in each of them. Over time, the nuts and bolts begin to corrode in the impure water, just like our character flaws will show up and corrode our life. People may not see them at first, but they will eventually permeate and corrupt our life so it becomes dirty and tainted; these impurities will reveal our true character.

You see, without Jesus Christ, our "goodness" is only manufactured in imperfection, and those flaws will eventually come to light. To become like Christ—the ultimate example of a perfect character—we must receive Him as our Lord and Savior. Then He can work in us to be transformed into His likeness, not before.

If you haven't trusted Christ, our prayer is that you will accept Him as your Savior right now. It's very simple. Just say out loud or silently in your heart, "Dear Jesus, I am a sinner. I believe you died on the cross for my sins. I need your forgiveness. Please be Lord of my life. Thank you for cleansing me and beginning your work in my life to make me more like you. Amen."

This is the legacy we want to leave to our children and why we take the time to bless them with a special vacation of their own—to remind them as they are becoming adults to continue to pursue Christ and His character in their lives. We have no possessions or positions of honor we can leave to our children when we're gone—only the truth that can mold their lives and character, to take them through whatever they may face and raise them above it.

THE SIX CORE VALUES

We all live by a set of values. Every decision we make is governed by what values we have chosen to control our lives. If our value is money, then the decisions we make today will be made with the idea of how to get more money or to keep the money we already have. If our value is helping others, we'll look for opportunities to help. Our job is to direct our children into making the right value choices they'll follow for the rest of their lives.

In the following chapters, we'll discuss the values we've chosen for our children. As we said earlier, you may not choose these exact values, or you may call them by another name. The important thing is that all these values are biblically based and serve to help us become more like Christ as we passionately pursue Him and strive to serve Him daily.

Don't measure yourself by what you have accomplished,
but by what you should have accomplished with your ability.

—*John Wooden*

Each value chapter will start with a description of the core value and its foundation in biblical principles, including a biblical person as an illustration. Next we'll discuss how to model this value with our own lives and how to teach this value to our children. We'll give you age-appropriate activities with each value. Finally, we'll explain the question and gift that we chose to signify this value on our Legacy Trips. We chose a question to go with each value that would make that particular value stick in our kids' minds and challenge them to abide by it. We also attach a gift to each value. This is something they can put in their room or carry with them—forever—that's a tangible reminder of the instilled value. Visual reminders can sometimes be the best way to keep us mindful of where we have been and where we are going. (A practical suggestion here: When you find a gift you like, go ahead and purchase one for each of your children and maybe even one for yourself so you have a set. Just store them away until the child's Legacy Trip because it may be difficult to find that exact item again a few years later.) You may choose different gifts than we did; customize the ideas to your family and style.

The main idea during the Legacy Trip is to focus on one value a day and have some way to remember them when you get home. You decide the best way for you and your children to do that. Jerolyn's favorite one is the question. All the questions are hanging on the wall in our kitchen. We have been known to use them when disciplining to remind our children of the core value their behavior is not living up to. It's quick, easy, and they know exactly what we're talking about and what they need to do to correct the behavior. These core values put everyone in your family on the same page and set your growing child, soon to be an adult, in a "win" situation. We truly want to send them off fully equipped to face the world and its responsibilities as whole and holy adults.

For Raising Christ Followers

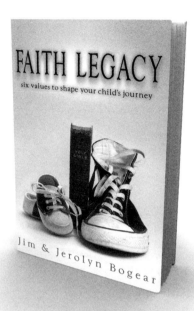

All parents want to pass on something of value to their children, but often we think primarily in financial terms. Much more valuable than the wealth, power, and financial security that the world craves, you can pass on to your children a legacy of faith. In this easy-to-read, highly practical book, veteran parents Jim and Jerolyn Bogear share their secrets for instilling godly character and values in their children. Having taken each of their three children on a Legacy Trip to reinforce the values they'd been teaching them, the authors outline the six biblical values—devotion, integrity, purity, positive attitude, generosity, and significance—that will help your children lead healthy, productive, and holy lives.

Faith Legacy
Six Values to Shape Your Child's Journey
By Jim and Jerolyn Bogear

Price: $16.99 (hardcover)
ISBN: 978-0-89827-427-1

Get started raising Christ Followers!

wesleyan
publishing
house
www.wphonline.com
800.493.7539

For more information, go to
www.wesleyan.org/catalog.